LOST RAIL\
OF
SHROPSHIRE

Best Wishes
Leslie Oppitz

LOST RAILWAYS
OF
SHROPSHIRE

Leslie Oppitz

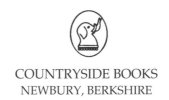

COUNTRYSIDE BOOKS
NEWBURY, BERKSHIRE

The cover picture shows GWR lcoomotive 4-6-0 no. 6960
Raveningham Hall hauling an express train through Gobowen
station in the mid 1940s and heading for Chester.
(From an original painting by Colin Doggett)

Designed by Mon Mohan
Maps by Brian Butler and Jennie Collins

Produced through MRM Associates Ltd., Reading
Printed by Woolnough Bookbinding Ltd., Irthlingborough

CONTENTS

ACKNOWLEDGEMENTS

Acknowledgements go to the numerous libraries and record offices throughout Shropshire and many of the surrounding areas who have delved into records. Thanks also to the late J. L. Smith of Lens of Sutton, D. K. Jones, Russell Mulford, John H. Meredith, Mark Hoofe, Alan Binns, John Joyce and Mark Smith for their help in providing many old and new photographs.

Thanks also go to the following who generously contributed with information: William Jack of Market Drayton; Ken Lucas, Hon. Secretary of the Bishop's Castle Railway Society; Ralph Cartwright, Vice President of the Welshpool & Llanfair Railway Preservation Society; Bill Lloyd, General Secretary, Shropshire Railway Society; Ian Rutherford, Hon. Treasurer & Director, Foxfield Railway; Dave Angell of the Telford Horsehay Steam Trust; Henry Thomas and Brian Rowe of the Cambrian Railways Trust, and Russell Mulford, Railway Photographer.

Personal thanks go to my wife, Joan, for travelling around Shropshire with me and also for her careful checking of the final manuscript.

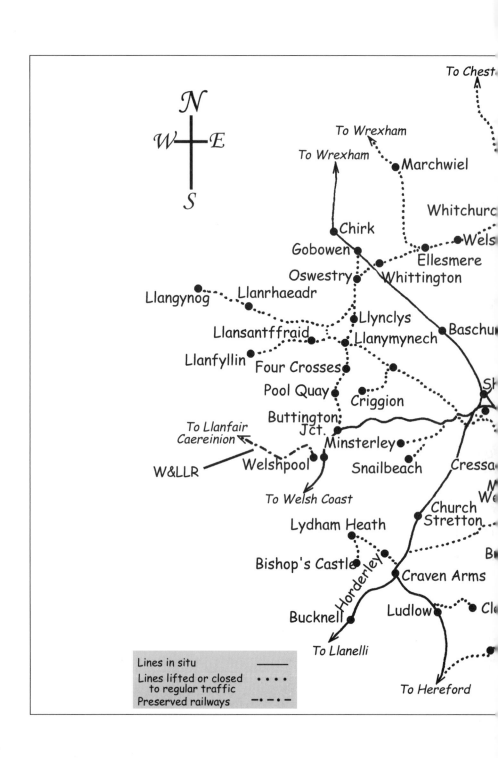

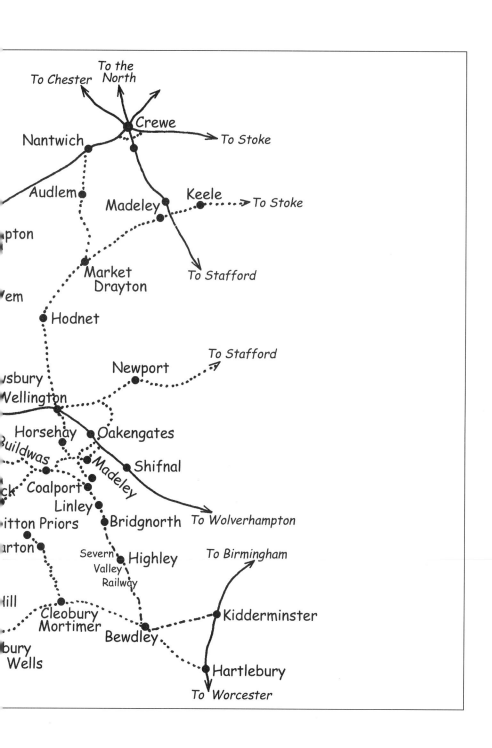

ABBREVIATIONS

The following abbreviations are used in this book:

BCR	Bishop's Castle Railway
BR	British Rail
CM&DPLR	Cleobury Mortimer & Ditton Priors Light Railway
GVT	Glyn Valley Tramway Company
GWR	Great Western Railway
HST	Horsehay Steam Trust (Telford)
LMS	London, Midland & Scottish Railway
LNWR	London & North Western Railway
LSWR	London & South Western Railway
NSR	North Staffordshire Railway
O&NR	Oswestry & Newtown Railway
OE&WR	Oswestry, Ellesmere & Whitchurch Railway
S&BR	Shrewsbury & Birmingham Railway
S&HR	Shrewsbury & Hereford Railway
S&MLR	Shropshire & Montgomeryshire Light Railway
SDR	Snailbeach District Railways
SUR&CC	Shropshire Union Railways & Canal Company
SVR	Severn Valley Railway
S&W	Shrewsbury & Welshpool Railway
THST	Telford Horsehay Steam Trust
TVLR	Tanat Valley Light Railway
WD	War Department
WM&CQR	Wrexham, Mold & Connah's Quay Railway
W&SJR	Wellington & Severn Junction Railway

Please note that:
'Junction' implies a railway station
'junction' means where railway lines meet

Introduction

When the railways came in the early 19th century it seemed that the drudgery of travel along poor roads and the slowness of canal traffic would be at an end. But this great new idea had its opponents. An article written in 1836 read: 'I foresee what the effect will be – it will set the world a-gadding. Twenty miles an hour! Why, you will not be able to keep an apprentice boy at work; every Saturday evening he must take a trip to spend the Sabbath with his sweetheart. Grave plodding citizens will be flying about like comets. All local attractions will be at an end.'

History tells us of course this was far from the truth. Conventional railways as known today began in 1825 with the establishment of the Stockton & Darlington Railway. The well-known Rainhill trials were held in 1829 on the Liverpool & Manchester Railway and won by George Stephenson's famous locomotive *Rocket*. Travelling was pretty uncomfortable in those early days, with railway carriages beginning as stage-coach bodies attached to wagon bases. They were small, cramped, unlit and had no heating or travel facilities.

Shrewsbury celebrated the arrival of trains on 12th October 1848, when a line from Shrewsbury to Chester opened officially. Shops were shut and church bells rang all day. It is recorded that to celebrate the opening the first train was made up of 39 coaches with over 1,000 people on board and it was hauled by three locomotives. Great crowds turned out to wave and cheer as it passed. Unfortunately when the train arrived at Chester all was not well. No reception had been organised for the party and there was 'neither a biscuit to eat nor a glass with which one could hob nob with another'! By the time the train was ready to return to Shrewsbury it must have been quite a spectacle. Another twenty carriages had been added and two more engines were needed to pull it. Following the failure of a reception at Chester, it was now running two hours late.

In June 1849 trains from Shrewsbury reached Oakengates and

a line opened from Wellington to Stafford. On 20th April 1852 the Shrewsbury & Hereford Railway reached Ludlow but there were delays for the railway to be completed. Trains eventually arrived at Hereford from Shrewsbury in December 1853.

From these major routes, branch lines developed where steam trains made their way across open stretches of countryside, linking remote villages and towns. In numerous instances passenger traffic remained light throughout, although goods or mineral traffic provided essential services. Some lines suffered an early demise simply because they became uneconomic, and, with road transport fast competing, the Beeching cuts of the early 1960s also took their toll.

This book, *Lost Railways of Shropshire*, examines the lives of the many 'lost' lines in and around Shropshire as well as their decline and closure. It provides the reader with a means to explore the numerous closed stations that can be found and the many trackbeds that have survived, some converted to footpaths. It also includes the preserved lines and societies of today that are dedicated to keeping the past alive.

Leslie Oppitz

1
Cambrian Railways: Lines to Oswestry and Wrexham and a Short GWR Branch

Whitchurch/Ellesmere/Oswestry
Ellesmere/Wrexham
Oswestry/Gobowen
Cambrian Railways Society/
Cambrian Railways Trust

Whitchurch station not long before its closure to Cambrian Railway traffic in January 1965. The station survives of course in a much reduced state on the Crewe-Shrewsbury line. (Lens of Sutton)

The Cambrian Railways came into being on 25th July 1864, when a number of smaller companies in Shropshire and North Wales amalgamated and established a headquarters at Welshpool. In 1866 the company decided to move its office and headquarters from Welshpool to Oswestry. Meantime a railway works had been built at Oswestry so that from the start the company used its own rolling stock and therefore carried out its own maintenance. As a result of the works, which cost £28,000 to build, Oswestry developed into an important railway centre and the town's population grew steadily.

Passenger services were slow to build up and opportunities were missed through directors' disagreements. In 1884 a receiver was appointed but this proved to be the company's saving, for within a number of years the company was on a better footing. Tourist traffic slowly built up, particularly to places such as Aberystwyth and Barmouth, both fast becoming boom towns.

Welshampton station on the Whitchurch-Oswestry line. There was a serious accident at Welshampton in June 1897, when eleven people died. (Lens of Sutton)

One of the companies that formed the Cambrian Railways was the Oswestry, Ellesmere & Whitchurch Railway (OE&WR), which had been planned as an important link between the London & North Western Railway's (LNWR) Shrewsbury-Crewe line and eventually the Welsh coast.

The section from Whitchurch to Ellesmere opened to goods traffic in April 1863 and passenger services began on 4th May the same year. Travelling the line from Whitchurch, trains reached the stations of Fenn Bank and Bettisfield. Because of strong opposition from certain landowners, particularly east of Ellesmere, the company was forced to build track across the swampy Fenn's Moss area.

On 11th June 1897 disaster struck when an excursion on its return journey from mid-Wales to Lancashire became derailed at Welshampton. Earlier that day a Cambrian Railways guard had complained that a small four-wheeled brake van was 'riding rough'. Despite this it was attached to the front of the train and Cambrian officials claimed at the subsequent inquest that it was this vehicle which caused the crash. The inspecting officer thought differently, blaming the speed of the train over track which in the Welshampton area needed renewal. Eleven people died in the accident.

Numerous ideas were put forward for a line between Ellesmere and Wrexham during the latter part of the 19th century. The Manchester, Sheffield & Lincolnshire Railway worked with the Cambrian Railways towards an agreement with the Mid-Wales Railway to provide an independent line between Birkenhead and the South Wales coalfields. Two links were required to complete the route. One was between Connah's Quay (near Queensferry) and Bidston on the Wirral and the other was between Wrexham and Ellesmere.

The Wrexham, Mold & Connah's Quay Railway (WM&CQR) opened in October 1888 but there were delays in building the section between Wrexham and Ellesmere. Parliament agreed the line in July 1885 but it was to be another ten years before services commenced. The first sod was cut on 11th July 1892 and the line was inspected in October 1895. There were three intermediate stations, Bangor-on-Dee, Overton-on-Dee and Marchwiel. The

12½ mile branch was single and each station had two platforms with passing loops. New platforms and a footbridge were built at Wrexham (Central) station, originally the WM&CQR terminus.

Services began on 2nd November 1895 and the line was worked by Cambrian Railways from the start. Cambrian trains were never worked beyond Wrexham Central station but this was no problem since connections were made with WM&CQR trains. Also the Central station was conveniently close to the town's shopping centre. Early locomotives were 4-4-0 side tanks, and for many years the branch was a busy one.

In September 1896 a half-mile double-tracked loop was constructed to avoid a reverse at Ellesmere so that trains could have a through run from Wrexham to Oswestry. It remained unused for a number of years but it reopened in 1911 to provide a through service from Manchester via Wrexham to Aberystwyth. During the First World War the service was diverted through Crewe but when the war ended the trains never returned.

In 1914 halts were opened at Sesswick and Trench. When the Wrexham to Ellesmere branch was absorbed by the GWR in 1923 a further halt opened at Hightown. Others followed in the 1930s at Cloy, Elson and Pickhill. Such efforts to increase traffic did not prove successful and it was not until the Second World War that the line benefited when a Royal Ordnance Factory was built at Marchwiel. Passenger trains were suspended from 1940 to 1946 so that priority could be given to munitions traffic.

After the war, local industries replaced the munitions factory, but, with road competition steadily increasing, the railway lost much of its use. Passenger services came to an end on 10th September 1962 but freight traffic survived many more years. When the twice-weekly china clay trains between Abenbury brickworks and Wrexham ceased in 1981, the line closed for good.

Today there are few reminders of the branch. Wrexham Central station still exists, although relocated nearby in recent years. It has been built to accommodate a shopping development called Island Green. The former station platform no longer exists, having given way to a shopping complex. The line connects with

Wrexham Central, seen here in earlier times. The double tracks on the left were used by trains to Bidston (a service still surviving), and Ellesmere trains left from across on the right. There were some eight trains each way daily. (Lens of Sutton)

Marchwiel station, between Ellesmere and Wrexham, closed to passenger traffic in 1962. This part of the line was perhaps at its busiest when a Royal Ordnance Factory was built in the area during the Second World War. (Lens of Sutton)

Wrexham General station, where the platform area has been refurbished maintaining the station's traditional style. For many years older style second-class-only trains have made regular runs from Wrexham Central to Bidston on the Wirral, making numerous stops and taking just under the hour. At Marchwiel the trackbed at the end of Station Road has become a walkway where a search in the undergrowth reveals traces of the former station. Abutments of the river Dee bridge at Bangor-on-Dee have survived, although the station has gone. The former goods yard is a coal yard. Overton-on-Dee was sited well over a mile from the village, and a sawmill covers much of the station area. At Ellesmere the former station area is an industrial site but the station building has survived.

Completion of the Ellesmere-Oswestry section was delayed by legal problems but it eventually opened on 27th July 1864. Intermediate stations included Frankton and Whittington (high-level). Frankton station has survived today as a private

Ellesmere once had a fine station building where trains could be caught to Oswestry, Whitchurch or Crewe. The building survives today in commercial use. In the 1920s, there were eight trains daily, with some providing a direct service to London Euston. (Lens of Sutton)

18

Frankton station between Ellesmere and Oswestry, c.1910. The building survives today as a private residence, still retaining the Cambrian Railways' coat of arms. (Lens of Sutton)

Whittington at one time had two stations. This upper station has long since been completely demolished. (Lens of Sutton)

residence. Whittington (high-level) station has been completely demolished and the embankment on the east side of the existing 'live' line between Gobowen and Shrewsbury has given way to a modern housing estate. But Station House is still there, a private residence called 'High Level Station House', and the road has been named Cambrian Avenue. There has been talk over the years about reopening Whittington (low-level) station on the Shrewsbury to Chester line but many difficulties still exist, including the need to acquire land for the station access.

Oswestry became an important rail junction as well as having a busy railway works. It was reached in 1848, first by a short branch linking the town with Gobowen on the main Shrewsbury to Chester line. Oswestry station opened in 1848, known as Oswestry GWR. When Cambrian line trains from Welshpool reached the town in 1860, a second station was built, known as

Oswestry station – a general view taken in 1954. The station building has survived and Somerfields supermarket and car park have been built to the right. This picture was taken from the footbridge which once carried employees across to the important Cambrian Railways Works.
(Lens of Sutton)

A GWR class 1400 no. 1416 locomotive seen at Oswestry on 16th September 1948. This locomotive, designed by C. B. Collett, was built in 1932. (John H. Meredith)

Oswestry Cam. The short branch to Gobowen had one intermediate station, this being Park Hall Halt, situated close to today's orthopaedic hospital. Many ex-soldiers today may well remember Park Hall since the area served as an army camp housing troops in transit to various war zones during two world wars. In 1924 the Oswestry GWR station closed and the Cambrian station handled all traffic. The Whitchurch to Oswestry line closed to passenger traffic on 18th January 1965 and the Oswestry to Gobowen branch followed on 7th November 1966.

When Gobowen station serving Shrewsbury to Chester trains was threatened with cutbacks, the station's booking office was taken over on 5th July 1993 by girls from nearby Moreton Hall School, ably led by David Lloyd, a former geography master at the school. They were initially based in the level-crossing keeper's cottage and did great work restoring the station and setting up a booking office plus a travel agency. On 7th March 1996 the running of the station was taken over by Severn-Dee Travel which continues today.

A train waits in the Gobowen bay at Oswestry in the early 1960s. The short branch closed on 7th November 1966. (Lens of Sutton)

The last passenger train to steam out of Oswestry was hauled by the 4-6-0 GWR locomotive no. 7822 *Foxcote Manor*. It was withdrawn from service the following year, and after, spending many years at a scrapyard in South Wales it was bought in 1975 for £5,000 to return to Oswestry (by road transport) to become an attraction at the home of the Cambrian Railway Society. The locomotive currently resides – fully restored and working – at the site of the Llangollen Railway Society.

Cambrian Railways Society

Looking to the future, numerous locomotives and items of rolling stock can be found at the Cambrian Railways Society, not far from the former Oswestry station. Items include a signal box from a goods yard at Llansantffraid , a station formerly on the branch from Llanymynech to Llanfyllin. Today the signal box is

Locomotive no. 7822 Foxcote Manor *photographed at Oswestry Depot on 27th August 1961. This Manor class 4-6-0 locomotive spent its whole working life in Shropshire, Cheshire and north and mid Wales. (Mark Hoofe)*

The last passenger train to steam out of Oswestry was hauled by the 4-6-0 GWR locomotive no. 7822 Foxcote Manor. *It is photographed here, shortly after its second overhaul at Llangollen, coasting into Glyndyfrdwy station. (John Joyce)*

23

Gobowen station on the main Shrewsbury to Chester line in modern times. The name board 'Gobowen for Oswestry' has been recreated to recall past times. (Author)

Photographed at Llynclys near Oswestry, the locomotive Cogan Hall awaits extensive repairs at the Cambrian Railways Trust site. It is hoped that a shuttle service using a rail motor will commence over a 1,400 yards stretch during 2004. (Author)

Track laying in early 2004 at the Cambrian Railway Trust's Llynclys site. Volunteer Brian Rowe assists in the preparation of 1,400 yards of track towards Pant along the former Cambrian trackbed. (Author)

better known as 'The Whistle Stop', an on-site refreshment room.

The Society hopes that public transport services may one day return between Oswestry and Gobowen. It is possible that at some future date a Parry People Mover lightweight railcar could be set up to cover the stretch, and, during 2004, the Society is training drivers at the Chasewater Railway (near Brownhills, just off the A5), where a people mover car is undergoing tests. It is expected this car will ultimately move to Oswestry.

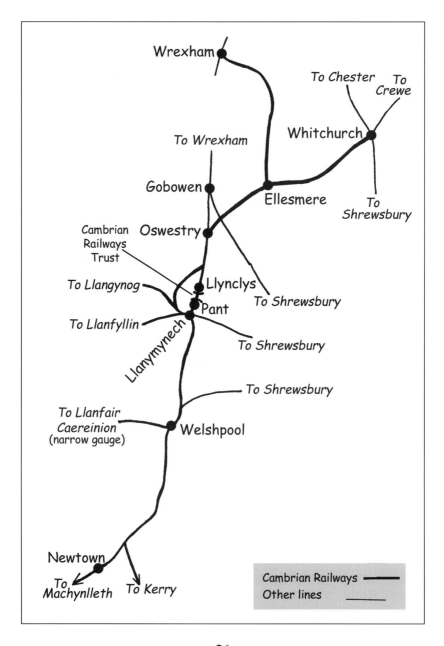

Cambrian Railways Trust

To the south of Llynclys there have been recent and important developments by the Cambrian Railways Trust. This followed a European grant of £307,000 given towards its Oswestry Heritage Steam Railway Project. Track and ballast have been acquired and it is planned to provide a shuttle service early in 2005 between Llynclys and Pen-y-Garreg Lane bridge in Pant, using a class 101 diesel multiple unit. Class 101s are the type (built in the late 1950s) which operated the Oswestry to Gobowen stretch in the early 1960s prior to closure of the line in 1966. The next aim of the Trust will be to provide run-round facilities at Llynclys station and then reinstate track from Llynclys station to link with a disused line still in existence between Oswestry and Blodwell Junction, thus aiming to eventually restore the link between Llynclys and Oswestry station.

Such projects depend on finance and a great deal of effort. Yet the Trust's plan is that one day soon trains will run again between Gobowen, Oswestry and Blodwell/Llanymynech. Exciting times are ahead.

2

A Cambrian Line towards Newtown and a Preserved Line

Oswestry/Welshpool/Newtown
Welshpool & Llanfair Light Railway

Llanymynech station, August 1935. An ex-Cambrian Railways 0-6-0 locomotive no. 893 arrives from Oswestry bound for Welshpool. On the right, remnants of the Potts line which closed to passengers in 1933. (Russell Mulford)

Oswestry/Welshpool/Newtown

On 26th June 1855, Parliament approved plans submitted by the Oswestry & Newtown Railway (O&NR) for a line to be built between Oswestry and Welshpool. Just over two years later, in August 1857, the ceremony of the cutting of the first sod by Lady Williams-Wynn was an opportunity for celebration. After the firing of guns at Powys Castle, a procession took place which included a wheelbarrow of solid mahogany carrying the company's crest.

On 1st May 1860 passenger services commenced between Oswestry and Pool Quay. Pool Quay to Welshpool followed on 14th August 1860, making possible an Oswestry to Welshpool service of six trains each way daily and two on Sundays. Doubling of the track was agreed by the Board of Trade in 1862 between Buttington and Welshpool, and between Oswestry and

An almost deserted platform at Llynclys, on the Cambrian main line between Oswestry and Llanymynech, not long before closure of the line. (Lens of Sutton)

Llanymynech in 1864. Buttington station opened with the Shrewsbury & Welshpool line in 1862, and at Llanymynech a platform was added in 1866 to serve the 'Potts line' (see Chapter 4).

Southwards from Oswestry, the first station was Llynclys. Just before the station, a Cambrian Railways mineral branch to Porth-y-waen left the main line. This branch was subsequently used in 1904, when a line was built along the Tanat valley to Llangynog (Chapter 3). Llynclys station building has survived today converted to a private residence. Next came Pant where all signs of the station have completely disappeared. The buildings and platform have gone, and the adjacent canal has all but dried up, although there are plans that this should be restored at some stage. At Pant only the name Station Road recalls the past. But trains are returning along a stretch of track relaid between Llynclys and Pant, following restoration carried out by the Cambrian Railways Trust – see Chapter 1.

Pant station in the early 1960s. The buildings and platform have all gone, and the adjacent canal has all but dried up. Only the name Station Road seems to have survived. (Lens of Sutton)

Staff pose at Four Crosses station in early steam days. Since closure the station has been totally demolished, with only a goods shed remaining. (Lens of Sutton)

Pool Quay in the early 1960s. The station has been demolished and the trackbed was used to straighten a section of the busy A483. (Lens of Sutton)

31

Llanymynech was a busy junction. Apart from the through train services, trains also left for Shrewsbury via the Potts line and also for Llanfyllin. Llanymynech station closed completely in January 1965. After crossing the river Vyrnwy, trains reached Four Crosses, where today only a goods shed remains, standing among buildings constructed on the station site by a former local creamery. At Arddleen the station building and platform edge give evidence of where trains once existed but at Pool Quay all signs have gone. The destruction of Pool Quay station gave road planners a chance to straighten out a short section of the adjacent A483.

After Buttington, where tracks met those from Shrewsbury, Welshpool was not far distant. The 'French Renaissance' style Welshpool station building has survived but in mid-1992 the existing track, Shrewsbury to Newtown and beyond, was realigned to a single island platform just to the east – a poor imitation of its former self. The original station trackbed has become part of the Welshpool bypass. Truly the trains have given way to the motor car. The original station building has become an Edinburgh Woollen Mill shop. Inside, many photographs recall the earlier days of steam, together with items of memorabilia competing with sound effects of trains arriving at the platform.

Travelling further southwards into Wales, Montgomery is followed by Abermule. Just to the south of the station tragedy struck in 1921, when two passenger trains collided head-on. One was a stopping train from Whitchurch and the other the Aberystwyth to Manchester express. Fifteen people were killed, including Lord Herbert Vane-Tempest, a director of the Cambrian Railway Company.

Newtown, described as the largest community in the old county of Montgomeryshire, was in fact a new town in the 14th century, when Roger de Moretimer was granted a right to hold a weekly market and two fairs a year there. Today the town is an important industrial centre, and its station survives on the main Shrewsbury to Aberystwyth and Pwllheli lines.

This is what happened when two passenger trains collided head-on at Abermule. Fifteen people were killed and such was the wreckage it took over 50 hours to clear the line. (Author's collection)

Newtown, c.1910. Today the town is an important industrial centre and the station survives on the main Shrewsbury–Aberystwyth/Pwllheli line. (Lens of Sutton)

Welshpool & Llanfair Light Railway

Had the parish councils of Llanfair during the years 1895-96 had their way then the railway from Llanfair would have linked with Arddleen by standard gauge along the Meifod Valley. The proposal was supported by 11 out of 12 local parishes.

It was the proposal by Welshpool Town Council supported by Castle Caereinion Parish Council that finally came to fruition, visualising narrow gauge tracks connecting with Welshpool, and only after a public inquiry to solve the controversy. One of the problems was that the cost of a narrow gauge line could not be raised locally and public funds had to be secured. The final cost was double a first estimate of £25,000.

The Welshpool & Llanfair Light Railway, worked by the Cambrian Railways, opened in 1903. It was built primarily for the carriage of agricultural requirements, although passenger traffic proved useful. On the official opening day there were

Single track at Arddleen station on the Oswestry to Welshpool line. Today the platform edge has survived and Station House has become a private residence. According to records, this station could have linked with a line from Llanfair had early planners had their way. (Lens of Sutton)

34

Beyer-Peacock locomotives **The Earl** *and* **The Countess** *stand by sheds at the Welshpool & Llanfair Light Railway, probably in the early 1950s, in pre-preservation days. Both locomotives are active on the Welshpool & Llanfair Railway today. (Lens of Sutton)*

Hunslet 2-6-2T no. 14/85 (ex-Sierra Leone Railway) runs round coaches at Welshpool Raven Square. Following a recent overhaul, the locomotive is currently in service at the Welshpool & Llanfair Light Railway. (Author)

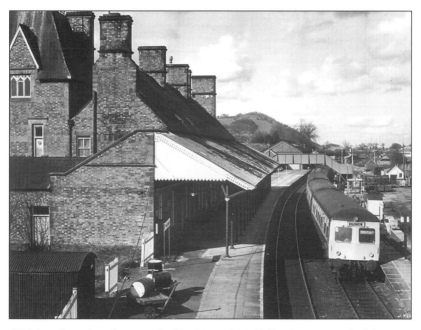

Welshpool station photographed in May 1984. Following removal of the track and station to the right to make way for a Welshpool bypass in 1993, the original station building has become an Edinburgh Woollen Mill establishment. (Russell Mulford)

great celebrations and in the years that followed local people packed the trains each market day. On railway grouping in 1923, ownership passed to the Great Western Railway, which then introduced a competing bus service. On 7th February 1931 the line closed to passenger traffic. Goods traffic continued to flourish for a time, including coal, builders' materials, cattle food, fertiliser, flour and many other supplies. Sheep and cattle were carried in both directions. The line prospered during the Second World War when petrol was scarce but afterwards traffic declined. The line became part of the nationalised British Railways in 1948 and closed completely in 1956.

But this was not the end. Already enthusiasts were ready to restore the line and four years later, in 1960, the Welshpool &

The Countess, *a Beyer-Peacock 0-6-0T locomotive, in steam at Welshpool Raven Square. The occasion was a 'special' run for enthusiasts (in wagons) between July 1949 and March 1951. (Lens of Sutton)*

Llanfair Light Railway Preservation Company Ltd was formed. Protracted negotiations followed and on 6th April 1963 a section opened between Llanfair Caereinion and Castle Caereinion. The formal opening was carried out by the Earl of Powis, and passenger trains ran again – the first for over 32 years. Any hopes of restoring the former link with the main line Welshpool station were dashed because trains were now barred from the town's streets. Many years of fundraising, rebuilding and hard work followed, with trains finally being restored to Welshpool on 18th July 1981, where a station was built at Raven Square. Today's fine station building, erected during 1992, came from Eardisley, where it once served the Hereford, Hay & Brecon Railway.

3

Branches into Wales

Llanymynech/Llanfyllin
Porth-y-waen/Blodwell Junction/Llangynog

Llanfyllin station in the 1940s. The 8½ mile branch from Llanymynech closed in January 1965. Today the platform building is in commercial use. (Lens of Sutton)

Llanymynech/Llanfyllin

Following the opening of the Oswestry & Newtown Railway (O&NR) from Oswestry to Welshpool in 1860, Llanfyllin, a market town set in the deep wooded valley of the river Cain in the Berwyn foothills, saw the opportunity for a rail link with Oswestry. A previous proposal for a narrow gauge Llanfyllin and Llangynog light railway had been defeated, as was a West Midland Railway scheme to open a line through to the Welsh coast via Llanfyllin by tunnelling through the Berwyn mountains. Parliament approved the 8½ mile branch from Llanymynech to Llanfyllin on 17th May 1861. Submitted by the O&NR (part of Cambrian Railways from 1864), the branch opened on 17th July 1863, with through services to Oswestry.

A journey between Llanymynech and Llansantffraid, initially the only intermediate station on the branch, was not without its difficulties. At Llanymynech trains had to reverse from a north-end bay, after which another change of direction was necessary. This was due to the proximity of the Montgomeryshire Canal, so a shunting neck was constructed, known as Rock Siding. Further stations on the branch followed in 1866 at Llanfechain and Bryngwyn. The latter was at first a 'flag stop', since, on Tuesdays and Wednesdays only, intending passengers had to work a signal on the platform to stop trains. It was later raised to the status of station.

Bryngwyn on the Llanfyllin branch not long before closure. For a time it was a 'flag stop' where passengers had to work a signal on the platform to stop trains. (Lens of Sutton)

39

The Llanfyllin Railway had a rather unexciting existence for most of its life even though it lasted for over a century. From 1881 Llanfyllin acquired importance as a railhead when large quantities of equipment arrived for the construction of Liverpool Corporation's Vyrnwy reservoir. Vast amounts of cement and iron pipe-work were delivered from Aberdovey harbour on the Cardigan Bay coast. In January 1896 the reversal problem at Llanymynech was overcome when a ½ mile curve was opened, allowing a direct approach to the branch by using a section of the original Potts line (see Chapter 4). In 1938 Carreghofa halt was opened on this stretch.

From 1936 GWR class 74XX 0-6-0PT locomotives were intro-duced. Previously an 0-4-2T, introduced by the GWR for light branch work, had been a frequent sight along the Cain valley, usually hauling a Swindon-built twin set comprising two non-corridor brake coaches. The last steam train to work the line was hauled by Ivatt-designed BR class 2 locomotive no. 46506.

At Llanymynech the station nameboard told main-line

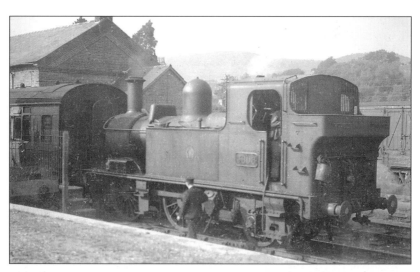

GWR 0-4-2T at Llanfyllin in the 1940s. The railway company claimed, 'Change at Llanfyllin for Lake Vyrnwy', not mentioning that a road journey of more than eight miles was needed! (Lens of Sutton)

travellers: 'Change for Llanfyllin and Lake Vyrnwy'. Nothing was said about the walk or perhaps ride by pony and trap of more than 8 miles from Llanfyllin that was necessary to reach the latter.

At Llanfyllin the terminus was quite substantial. Dominated by a large Victorian building (still in commercial use today), it had a single platform with a run-round loop and a large yard with numerous buildings. A significant part of the goods traffic comprised sheep and lambs. Freight traffic came to an end on the Llanfyllin branch in 1964, all traffic ceasing from 18th January 1965, the same day that Oswestry to Welshpool services terminated. With so little traffic on these lines, they could hardly be expected to be spared.

Llansantffraid station building lives on as the popular Station Restaurant. Opened in 1968, three years after closure of the line, extensive alterations have been made. Today customers can still savour the atmosphere of the old station, sitting where once passengers waited for a train perhaps to Oswestry market or to do their shopping. In the restaurant many pictures of the branch

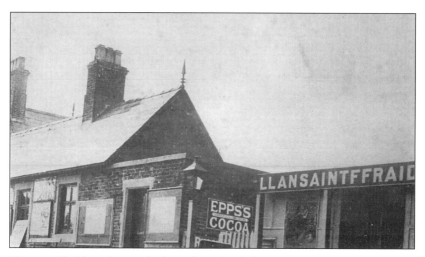

Llansantffraid station on the branch to Llanfyllin, c. 1910. The building is now the popular Station Restaurant. (Lens of Sutton)

41

recall the past, timetables are preserved and even the station clock is on show. The restaurant is a must for train enthusiasts and non-enthusiasts alike.

Porth-y-waen/Blodwell Junction/ Llangynog

The attractive village of Llangynog at the foot of the Berwyns came into prominence with the development of lead and slate working in the area. Lead mines on Craig Rhiwarth were discovered in 1692, and in the early 18th century a vein of almost pure galena (a source of lead ore) was found. As transport improved in the mid-19th century, Llangynog came close to pro-minence once again when a railway was planned in 1860, putting the village on the through route of a proposed West Midlands, Shrewsbury and coast of Wales railway. To proceed it

Looking east at Blodwell Junction, where Potts Line freight to and from Nantmawr met Tanat Valley trains. If today's railway planners have their way, trains could return to Blodwell Junction at some future date. (Lens of Sutton)

was necessary to tunnel through the Berwyns but, when the high cost to achieve this was realised, the idea was dropped.

With Llangynog's mining activities hampered by the need for adequate transport to carry the ores to the smelting works (one was at Pool Quay), inevitably numerous ideas for branch lines followed but it was to be many more years before such a proposal was achieved. It took the Light Railway Act of 1896 to expedite matters and by the following year two plans were being considered. Firstly a proposal came from the Llanfyllin & Llangynog Light Railway for a 2 ft 6 ins gauge line to be built from the Cambrian Railways terminus at Llanfyllin. The other came from the Tanat Valley Light Railway (TVLR) for a standard gauge line to link Llangynog with the existing Porth-y-waen mineral branch. The Porth-y-waen branch had opened in 1861 to serve limestone quarries and ran from Porth-y-waen junction (just north of Llynclys) on the Cambrian Railways main line.

Local feeling favoured the standard gauge line. It was considered this would not only provide an adequate outlet for the quarries but cater for people travelling to Oswestry. In addition, trains could carry further pipes needed at the Vyrnwy reservoir. The Board of Trade confirmed a Light Railway Order for the standard gauge Tanat Valley Railway on 4th January 1899.

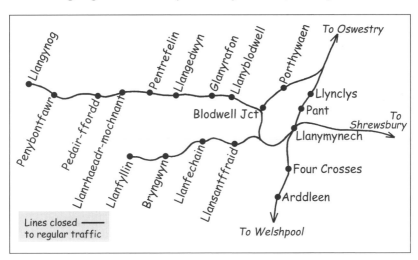

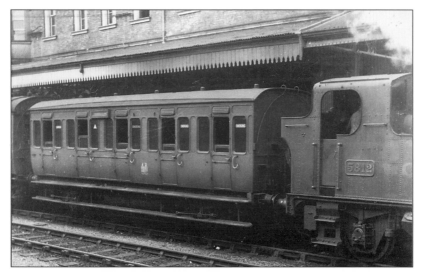

*A Tanat Valley branch train at Oswestry, September 1948. GWR 0-4-2T
class 1400 no. 5812 hauls a passenger set including 4-wheeled coach no. 15.
(John H. Meredith)*

The ceremony of cutting the first sod took place on 12th
September 1899 in a large field at Porth-y-waen, where a
grandstand covered with bunting had been erected. Close by,
stood a big marquee 'bulging with food for the luncheon to
follow', an event that a local newspaper later described as 'the
jolliest bun-fight seen in the area for many a year'.

Construction of the line went ahead but there were many
problems. Apart from the perhaps predictable bad weather, the
contractor made slow progress. There was an occasion when the
directors paid an unexpected visit to the sites to find them
deserted and the navvies sacked. To make up lost time, work
was continued on Sundays, this bringing complaints from those
'grateful for the Sabbath'. Finance too was a problem and further
assistance came from the Treasury and local councils and also
Liverpool Corporation with its interest in the Lake Vyrnwy
reservoir.

At the formal opening of the TVLR on 5th January 1904, the Dowager Lady Williams-Wynn performed the ceremony at Porth-y-waen, where level crossing gates were closed across the track and secured by a silver chain and padlock. Lady Williams-Wynn opened the railway by unlocking the padlock with a gold key and the train, Cambrian four-wheeled coaches hauled by a Seaham tank locomotive class 2-4-0, left for Llangynog.

Public and goods services began the next day. The branch, worked by the Cambrian Railways, consisted of ten inter-mediate stations with Porth-y-waen junction being renamed Llynclys junction. A weekdays only service provided four trains daily between Oswestry and Llangynog. It was not long, however, before the TVLR ran into trouble. The costs of construction had proved to be double those of the original estimate and it was soon realised that traffic would not reach the levels expected. Within three months a receiver was appointed, a

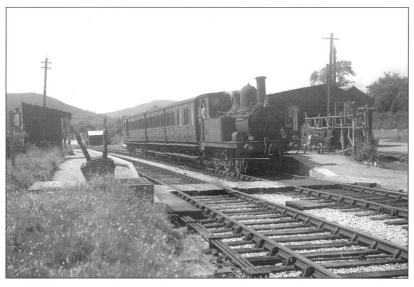

A GWR locomotive hauls an Oswestry-bound train at Llanrhaeadr in the late 1940s. The station was popular with walkers to the well-known Pistyll Rhaeadr waterfall over four miles away. (Lens of Sutton)

45

situation that was to remain until the Cambrian Railways took over the line in March 1921. The following year the Cambrian Railways formally became part of the GWR.

For many years the trains to Llangynog continued undisturbed along the quiet valleys. Track maintenance on the single-track branch was often neglected. More than once the leading wheels of the Seaham tank locomotives dropped between the rails where the track had spread, and a crowbar had to be carried to ease the wheels back onto the rails. The most important intermediate station was at Llanrhaeadr-ym-Mochnant, which possessed a crossing loop, two platforms and a platform building with the luxury of a separate ladies WC tacked on to the booking office/waiting room! In later years, as mineral traffic ceased, Llanrhaeadr served as a railhead in coal, lime, fertilisers and animal feedstuffs.

During the Second World War, the Tanat Valley reduced its passenger services but they were not increased again when the war ended. When a national coal shortage came in 1951, all

This is all that remained of Llangynog station after closure of the line in 1951. The station site is now a caravan park. (Lens of Sutton)

46

Llanyblodwell station on the Tanat Valley branch. Today the track has gone and the station building has gone, but the platforms survive and have been used to accommodate beehives. (Lens of Sutton)

services were 'withdrawn temporarily' but they were never to return. Passenger services ceased officially on 5th February 1951, to be replaced by road services operated by Crosville Motor Services Ltd. In July 1952 freight services were withdrawn between Llangynog and Llanrhaeadr and for a time the stretch of track accommodated disused wagons. In December 1960, following damage to a bridge caused by floodwater, the line between Llanrhaeadr and Blodwell Junction closed completely.

Today sections of the trackbed can be traced, although nearly all the stations have vanished. At Llangynog a short section of platform has survived in a caravan park. Remains of Llanyblodwell station can still be found but the platforms are adorned with beehives. Yet strange occurrences still happen. It is said that on clear moonlight nights at Llanyblodwell the figure of a platelayer makes its ghostly way along the trackbed!

4

The 'Potts' Line

Shrewsbury/Kinnerley/Llanymynech
Kinnerley/Criggion

The Potts line station at Llanymynech with staff posing by 'Gazelle'.
On the right the main line Cambrian station. (Lens of Sutton)

Just to the south of Kinnerley, where a railway junction once served local folk, providing trains to Shrewsbury, Llanymynech or even Criggion, there is a road bridge which formerly crossed the railway line. The trains have long since gone but the memories remain, for those were the days of the Shropshire & Montgomeryshire Railway, or the 'Potts line' as it became known. There were engines with such names as *Pyramus*, *Hesperus*, *Thisbe*, *Daphne* and *Dido*. Another, still remembered by many today, was *Gazelle*, nicknamed 'the Coffee Pot'. It was built at Kings Lynn in 1893 and brought to the Potts line in 1911.

48

The Potts line had a complex and undulating history. Its future could hardly have been considered prosperous, since it covered an area of scattered farmlands and small villages as well as crossing ground subject to periodic heavy flooding. Planned originally as the West Shropshire Mineral Railway, it was succeeded by the Shrewsbury & North Wales Railway, which was designed to leave the Shrewsbury to Welshpool line just to the south of Shrewsbury to reach Llanymynech, with a 3 mile extension from Llanymynech to Llanyblodwel to serve Nantmawr quarry. From Kinnerley a 6 mile branch was planned to the granite quarries at Criggion.

The proposals came to reality when the North Staffordshire Railway backed the venture, thus creating the Potteries, Shrewsbury & North Wales Railway – hence the nickname 'Potts'. It was also intended to carry passengers. However, plans to seek running powers over the existing main line into Shrewsbury General station were turned down by Parliament,

The Potts line was not allowed access to Shrewsbury's main station, so a terminus was built at Abbey Foregate. An LMS (ex-LNWR) locomotive waits to haul a passenger train to Llanymynech in the early 1930s. (Lens of Sutton)

so an independent approach had to be made with the building of Abbey Foregate station. The terminus was sited where the former Abbey refectory once stood. A pulpit (built in the late 14th century) remains railed off in the former station yard and scheduled as an ancient monument.

The line first opened on Monday, 13th August 1866, providing passenger services on double track between Shrewsbury and Llanymynech. No official ceremony took place, but the local people were not prepared to let such an occasion pass without note. According to the *Shrewsbury Chronicle*, large numbers of passengers in special excursion trains, from Shrewsbury arrived at Llanymynech where they either 'ascended Llanymynech Hill' or 'sought sport in the river Vyrnwy as well filled baskets testified'.

All did not go well, for the company soon ran into financial difficulties. It struggled on until 3rd December 1866 when the bailiffs moved in. In the book the *Shropshire & Montgomeryshire Light Railway*, Keith and Susan Turner wrote of an amusing tale

Looking westwards at Kinnerley Junction, where tracks left for Llanymynech or Criggion. The bay platform on the left was intended for Criggion trains. A railcar stands beyond the ground frame. (Lens of Sutton)

about a debenture holder who obtained a writ against the company. A train arriving at Abbey Foregate was seized but after much haggling it was allowed to leave with a bailiff on board. He was duly settled in a first-class compartment but on arrival at Llanymynech he was politely moved to another compartment set aside for him.

After calling at Kinnerley on the return journey, there was a short period of shunting. As the train left for Shrewsbury, the bailiff became suspicious and, looking out of the window, he saw the rest of the train disappearing into the distance. Arriving rather footsore at Shrewsbury after midnight, he was informed that a coupling chain had broken and his coach had been left behind – quite by accident!

Finance remained a problem, so traffic was suspended on 21st December 1866 until some of the company's assets could be realised. A plan was considered to amalgamate with a number of small Welsh railway companies but this was rejected. Another idea was to build a spur from Abbey Foregate station to connect with a proposed Market Drayton link, but again this did not happen.

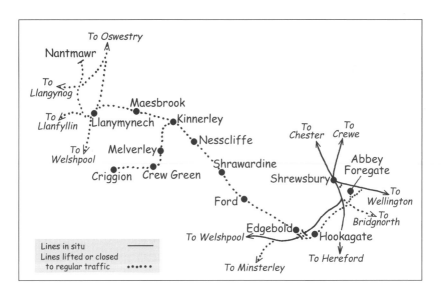

A lone passenger at Crew Green station on the Criggion branch. The platform was equipped solely with a former tramcar seat. View taken looking towards Melverley. (Lens of Sutton)

Eventually, in December 1868, services resumed but they were at a reduced level and the line had been singled. In 1871 a branch opened from Kinnerley to Criggion, mainly for freight, although there was some passenger traffic. Except for Melverley's brick structure, the few stations on the branch were initially wooden buildings and a wooden viaduct across the river Severn at Melverley was described as 'rickety'. The company benefited from additional freight traffic when a year later in 1872 a further branch extended beyond Llanymynech to Nantmawr, where ample limestone could be found. To reach Nantmawr, the company had to obtain agreement with the Cambrian Railways for running powers over their metals at Llanymynech.

Matters overall did not improve and finances continued to deteriorate. All possible economies were made and fares were reduced. In 1877 an official receiver was appointed, and in 1880 a 25 mph speed limit was imposed until the standard of the track was improved. This never happened and services were further cut back and later in 1880 all traffic was again suspended.

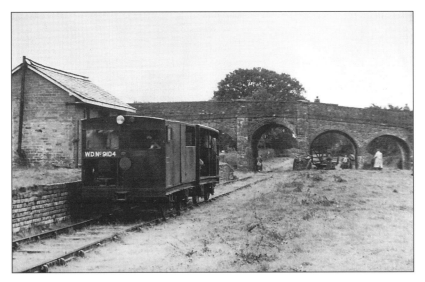

Melverley station, September 1958, during a visit by the Stephenson Locomotive Society. The excursion used two Drewry petrol railcars. The bridge has subsequently been demolished. (Lens of Sutton)

In 1881 the Cambrian Railways took over the line west of Llanymynech, with this short section reopening in 1886. A new company called Shropshire Railways emerged in 1890 and the track between Llanymynech and Shrewsbury was relaid. Once again, receivership followed and the buildings and other structures went into further decay. In 1902, the 'rickety' wooden viaduct over the Severn at Melverley collapsed.

Local pressure to reopen the line came in 1907 and the Shropshire & Montgomeryshire Light Railway (S&MLR) was formed, largely financed by local councils. A Light Railway Order was issued in February 1909 and work began to clear the track. Melverley viaduct was rebuilt and all the sleepers were replaced. The engineer was H. F. Stephens, later Colonel Stephens, well known for his light railway adventures elsewhere in the country. The line reopened on Maundy Thursday, 13th April 1911, when the Mayor of Shrewsbury, Major Wingfield, gave an opening speech from the top of a freshly painted ex-

Midland Railway coach to a large crowd. Later, an eight-coach special, hauled by 0-6-0 ex-LSWR *Hesperus*, left for Llanymynech amidst exploding detonators and loud cheering.

The Criggion branch reopened in February 1912 for freight and for passengers six months later. Over the next twenty years traffic remained at a low level, hardly surprising for such a thinly populated area with rural halts miles from anywhere. Sometimes trains from Shrewsbury were used by walkers or parties who wished to visit the surrounding countryside at Llanymynech or the Breidden Hills at Criggion.

In the 1920s, economies on the Potts line included experiments with Ford railcars, although these proved somewhat unpopular. They left passengers with a ringing in their ears from the noise created by the pressed steel wheels. An unusual vehicle pur-

In the 1920s economies became necessary on the Potts line and railcars were used. At Llanymynech a Ford lorry hauls a railcar. These became very unpopular and the rail cars became known as the 'rattlers'. (Russell Mulford)

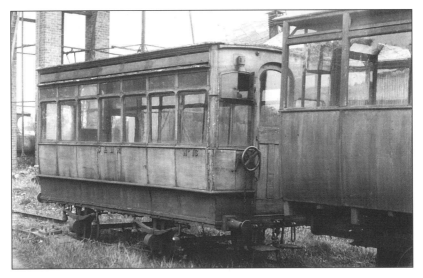

Among Col. Stephen's acquisitions was a tramcar, seen on the left, bought from London County Council and previously used as a horse-drawn vehicle. After removal of the top deck, stairs and various extras, it was converted for use by rail. (Lens of Sutton)

chased by Colonel Stephens and converted for use with *Gazelle* was a tramcar that originally had a double deck and was drawn by two horses in London. This was equally unpopular and became known as the 'rattler'.

When Colonel Stephens died in 1931, the line deteriorated further. In the following year, passenger trains on the Criggion branch ceased beyond Melverley, since the viaduct was once again considered unsafe, and £280 was spent on repairs. In November 1933 all regular S&MLR passenger services ceased and only excursions survived. In 1940 there were further bridge problems when ice flows carried away six piles. Repairs were completed by October 1941. Gradually, stations decayed and the weeds took over the track once again. Yet despite its apparent end, the line was to experience yet another lease of life.

In June 1941 the section from Shrewsbury to Llanymynech was requisitioned by the War Department (WD) to serve the

Shoot Hill in the late 1950s. The War Department relinquished control of the Potts line in 1960, and, apart from oil sidings at Shrewsbury, the track was lifted in 1962. (Lens of Sutton)

extensive ammunition depots which had been established throughout the area. Kinnerley yard became rife with khaki, and the sidings were full of military stock. Nissen huts sprang up like mushrooms, and yet again the line was relaid, this time with concrete sleepers. Before long, as many as twelve locomotives were in steam simultaneously. Numerous sidings served over 200 ammunition store buildings, the system worked by the No. 1 Group of the Royal Engineers.

During the war there was a limited number of trains for passengers or WD personnel, but services were always infrequent and unreliable. When a farmer from Dyffryd at Maesbrook drove up to the crossing one morning, he noticed that one pole was up and the other down. When he asked the lady crossing keeper why was this, she commented that she was 'half expecting a train'.

Towards the end of the war it became necessary to rebuild the up side of a viaduct at Shrawardine, where a pillar showed

Maesbrook station during the Second World War, when the line was used to serve the many ammunition depots in the area. (Lens of Sutton)

distinct signs of sagging. Royal Engineer personnel cut down the original girders and a Bailey bridge structure, able to take heavier loads, was placed on the remaining pillars. Shortly after the war, floods in the area were worse than usual, with water reaching the top of the embankment at Shrawardine. At the same time a bridge over a stream at Maesbrook was completely swept away, stranding a locomotive at Llanymynech.

In 1959 the WD closed its last depot, and in the same year the stone traffic by rail ceased from Criggion. In 1960 the line returned to civilian status and operations were gradually run down. The last scheduled train for civilian workers ran from Shrewsbury to Llanymynech on 26th February 1960 and on 29th February the line closed officially. A farewell trip by the Stephenson Locomotive Society took place in March. Shrawardine viaduct was dismantled in 1962, but Melverley viaduct on the already closed Criggion branch was rebuilt as a

Gazelle approaches Criggion station hauling a tramcar converted to a railway coach. Mineral trains travelled beyond Criggion to a processing plant and loading facility for transporting dolerite from Criggion Quarry. (Lens of Sutton)

road bridge. In the same year BR completed removal of all track apart from oil depot sidings at Shrewsbury, which had been connected to main line tracks in 1960.

The Potts line had at last been laid to rest, but many today recall the days of steam with affection. Many stations have become private residences. Kinnerley shed, which was refurbished by the WD in July 1941, is today in industrial use and the water tower, erected in 1958 to replace an earlier one, still stands close by. The locomotive *Gazelle* can be found at the Kent and East Sussex Railway at Tenterden in Kent.

A local from Maesbrook recalled a tale from his grandmother's days. Whilst travelling on the Potts line, the train, which ran slowly enough at the best of times, suddenly juddered to a halt. She leaned out of the window and shouted to the driver, 'What's up?' 'Sheep on the line,' came the reply. In a short while the train started again and then once more shuddered to a

Col Stephens bought Gazelle *in 1911, mainly for use on the Criggion branch. It was built in Kings Lynn in 1893 and can be seen today at the Kent & East Sussex Railway at Tenterden in Kent. (Lens of Sutton)*

A 'Dean goods' with freight passes Edgebold (formerly Hanwood Road) station, bound for Hookagate, in 1947. (Lens of Sutton)

halt. 'What's up this time?' shouted the impatient passenger. 'We've caught up the sheep,' came the driver's terse reply.

After a while the driver shouted back, 'Why don't you get out and walk – it could be quicker.' 'I can't do that,' she replied, 'I'm being met at the station and I said I'd be on this train . . .'

Throughout its existence, Shrewsbury's Abbey Foregate station had seemed insignificant compared with the General station. Passengers entered by the small gate on the left, the right hand side being a goods entrance. The station buildings comprised a booking office and, unusually for the Potts Line, a ladies' waiting room. During the Second World War this latter room was used by the ARP. Unfortunately for male travellers, no toilets were provided either on the trains or at stations anywhere along the line. Perhaps it was fortunate the trains made numerous unscheduled stops throughout their journey.

5

A Joint Line to Minsterley and a Mineral Branch

Shrewsbury/Pontesbury/Minsterley
Pontesbury/Snailbeach

At Minsterley there were four passenger trains daily on weekdays, although the branch was never heavily used. The line closed to passengers in February 1961. Today only the stationmaster's house beyond the station survives, as a private residence. (Lens of Sutton)

Shrewsbury/Pontesbury/Minsterley

A 9½ mile branch from Shrewsbury to Minsterley opened on 14th February 1861 with intermediate stations at Hanwood, Plealey Road and Pontesbury. The following year a line was built leaving the Minsterley branch beyond Hanwood to link with Welshpool and joining the Oswestry & Newtown Railway at Buttington. On 5th July 1865 the Welshpool and Minsterley branches became vested in the LNWR and the GWR jointly. Passenger traffic to Minsterley was never heavy, with four trains daily each way but none on Sundays. By the turn of the century this had improved to seven daily each way and one Sunday train each way. The journey lasted just over half an hour, taking passengers along the attractive Rea Brook valley and skirting Pontesford Hill. Apart from passenger services, the branch also attracted milk and agricultural goods, but it was the mineral traffic, which came down from the Stiperstones on the Snailbeach District Railways to an exchange point at Pontesbury, that kept the line profitable.

From April 1919 competition for passengers came from a bus service that began between Minsterley and Shrewsbury. The railway countered with various offers including through market

Plealey Road station on the Minsterley branch was little used, being in a very rural area. The platform building has become a private residence. (Lens of Sutton)

tickets and, for a time, it held its own. As an economy measure, trains from Minsterley were mixed freight and passenger. After grouping in 1922, the branch became GWR & LMS Joint and it was a familiar sight to see LMS (ex-LNWR) 0-6-2 tanks along the line. During the Second World War, passenger services enjoyed a new lease of life because petrol shortages meant that rural buses had to cut back.

The Minsterley branch finally fell victim to road competition, with closure to passenger traffic on 5th February 1951. The closure also came at a time when the country was suffering a coal crisis. Freight traffic survived another 16 years, until May 1967, and the track was finally lifted in 1973. The line from Shrewsbury to Welshpool still exists, of course, although Hanwood station, initially an intermediate station on the Minsterley branch, closed to passengers in 1960, when all the intermediate stations and halts on the Welshpool line closed.

At one time the terminus at Minsterley boasted a milk wharf, a goods shed, cattle and horse docks and numerous sidings.

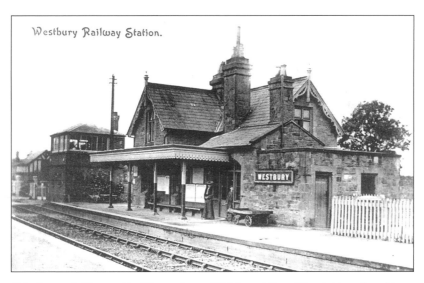

Westbury station on the Shrewsbury–Welshpool line. The station closed in September 1960. (Lens of Sutton)

*Passengers wait at Yockleton station and milk churns await collection
c.1910. Today no intermediate station exists between Shrewsbury and
Welshpool. (Lens of Sutton)*

During a recent visit, the author found a local resident who
recalled the GWR/LMS days. Starting work at Shrewsbury in
1927 as a parcel porter, he was transferred to Minsterley in 1947,
after the Second World War, as a freight checker, and he
remained there until closure. Station House has survived, but
little else. Today a private residence, the owner recalled the
trouble he had removing the base that had previously supported
a water tower. 'The concrete was four feet thick and it needed a
lot of hard work to remove it,' he reflected. 'When they did
things in those days, they did them properly!'

Pontesbury/Snailbeach

It is known that mining existed at the Stiperstones centuries ago
when the Romans obtained lead from shallow borings, and their
old workings can still be traced in the Hope district. Mining was

64

Mineral traffic on the Snailbeach Railway came to an end in the late 1950s when all available locomotives failed. For a time a diesel tractor was used straddling the track. (Lens of Sutton)

not taken seriously in the area until the 19th century, when a small number of moderately sized concerns came into existence. As business grew, so transport increased as a problem. Various schemes were put forward to run trains along the Rea valley but it was not until the standard gauge branch from Shrewsbury to Minsterley opened in February 1861 that rail transport became available.

It was because of this that the Snailbeach District Railways (SDR) came into existence. The company was incorporated by an Act of Parliament, dated 5th August 1873, which authorised two railways, each of 2 ft 4 ins gauge. The first was planned to run westwards from Pontesbury station (on the Minsterley branch) to Crowsnest, just beyond Snailbeach village. The second line was to be an extension of just under 2 miles, skirting the Stiperstones to reach lead mines at Pennerley. Finance proved difficult to attract, particularly since this was not intended to be a passenger carrying railway, and only the first railway was built.

Trains on the 2 ft 4 in gauge Snailbeach District Railway reached Crowsnest and then reversed up the side of the hill to the mines. (Lens of Sutton)

The village of Snailbeach owes its existence largely to the days of mining. Many of the dwellings go back to these earlier times, as do the local places of worship, the public houses (some now private properties) and two schools (one became a field centre). The miners were great sports enthusiasts marbles contests were regularly held and footballers were renowned for their robust play. Choirs were notable, with a popular slogan being 'Sing for lead, whistle for coal'.

When the narrow gauge SDR opened in 1877, its future seemed prosperous. The annual tonnage carried in the first five years averaged at 14,000, and shareholders benefited from a 3% dividend. Some 40 wagons were in use, hauled initially by 0-4-2ST *Belmont*, assisted later by 0-6-0ST *Fernhill*, delivered in 1881. The company's good fortune was not to last, for in 1884 the SDR suffered when one of its best customers, the Tankerville Great Consuls Company, closed its mines in Tankerville, Pennerley and The Bog. This had the effect of reducing the annual tonnage to around 5,500 annually.

The SDR seemed doomed to extinction but relief came when the Ceiriog Granite Company opened a quarry in 1905 on the north side of Eastridge Wood, near Habberley. A branch line was built to the quarry and during the following year over 20,000 tons of mineral traffic were carried. Extra power was needed and the Glyn Valley Tramway Company (GVT) made available *Sir Theodore*, a 0-6-0T built by Beyer Peacock. Unfortunately the GVT gauge was 2 ft 4½ ins and the flanges of *Sir Theodore* kept riding up the sides of the Snailbeach metals, so the engine had to be returned. A new locomotive was supplied in 1906, a six-coupled side tank with the name of *Dennis*.

By 1909 the annual tonnage reached 38,000, but this state of affairs was not to last and trade fell off once more. The First World War (1914–1918) further worsened the situation and trade continued to dwindle. Help came once again in 1923, when Colonel Stephens, a man renowned for his light railway exploits throughout the country, including the Potts line (see Chapter 4),

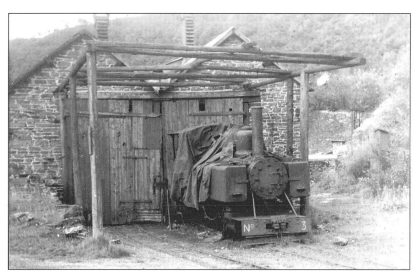

Locomotive WD538 no. 3, rebuilt and regauged from 1 ft 11½ ins to 2 ft 4 ins by Bagnall in 1918, photographed at Snailbeach in September 1948. (John H. Meredith)

Happily for posterity the Snailbeach locomotive shed still exists having been refurbished through the auspices of Shropshire County Council. Not far away, sections of track and points with their levers have survived the many years since closure. (Author)

took over. Efficiency improved at once, and, although lead traffic had virtually disappeared, a barytes mine had opened with a new quarry on Callow Hill.

In the book *The Snailbeach District Railways*, Eric S. Tonks wrote of the period in the 1920s when the line was almost entirely worked by a driver-cum-fitter by the name of Gatford, who had served earlier on the Bishops Castle Railway. Driver Gatford ran the SDR virtually single-handed, keeping the engines and wagons in working order with the limited resources available. At least he had no commuting problems. At the end of each day, after taking on coal and water, he would leave the engine on the track outside his garden gate ready for the next day's work.

Colonel Stephens died in 1931, and by the following year the SDR was entirely dependent on the quarry at Callow Hill for traffic. Under new management three further locomotives were purchased and quarrying continued. The SDR survived until 1947, when Shropshire County Council, lessees of the Callow Hill quarries, purchased the line. Traffic struggled on until 1959, when the last available locomotive failed and for a time a diesel farm tractor straddled the rails to haul wagons.

A visit to Snailbeach today can prove most rewarding. Located to the south of Minsterley and off the A488, a narrow road climbs to cross the redundant trackbed by a chapel. At a higher point a rough turning leads off to the left, where once existed numerous mines, and it is here that a locomotive shed, refurbished by Shropshire County Council, can be found.

6

Bishop's Castle Railway

Craven Arms/Stretford Bridge/
Lydham Heath/Bishop's Castle

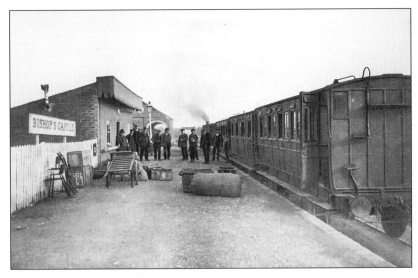

Assorted items await collection at Bishop's Castle station. The branch
opened in 1866, with four trains daily in each direction, usually mixed
passenger and freight. (Lens of Sutton)

The townsfolk of Bishop's Castle had long wanted a railway link
with 'the outside world'. Plans were deposited in 1860 and the
whole route was surveyed. The Bishop's Castle Railway (BCR)
was incorporated in June 1861, proposing a railway linking the
Oswestry & Newtown Railway at Montgomery with the
Shrewsbury & Hereford Railway at Wistanstow Halt (later to be
called Stretford Bridge) and then a branch via Lydham Heath to
Bishop's Castle.

A proposal was also under consideration from the competing Shrewsbury & Welshpool Railway to extend its newly-opened Minsterley branch through Chirbury to Bishop's Castle, providing a direct link with Shrewsbury. This latter plan received considerable backing from numerous tradespeople, who travelled to London to give their support. Unfortunately their journey was undertaken before consultation with several local prominent people (including a clergyman) who preferred the original Bishop's Castle Railway proposals. As a result, these same gentlemen immediately closed their accounts with the tradespeople concerned and the clergyman even asked that they should be excluded from his church!

Despite this opposing scheme, the Bishop's Castle Railway Bill received Royal Assent on 28th June 1861 agreeing a line from Montgomery to Wistanstow plus a branch from Lydham Heath (requiring a reversal) to Bishop's Castle, which gave a total length of 19½ miles. Final surveys and working plans were

Where Bishop's Castle trains once left the main line, photographed in July 1935, three months after closure. The branch failed through neglect and lack of passengers. (John H. Meredith)

71

completed during 1862 and negotiations to acquire the necessary land were put in hand.

Work by the contractor, Mr Savin, started in March 1863 but it was not long before there were serious delays. Apart from the lack of available finance, the BCR also had grave misgivings over Mr Savin. His company was clearly overstretching itself with additional involvements in construction work on the Cambrian Railways as well as the building of numerous hotels. A bill was filed in Chancery by the BCR to recover the sum of £20,500 already advanced, and a new contractor, Mr G. M. Morris of Plowden, was appointed. Many had given up hope that the line would ever be built. Work eventually started on 24th October 1864 on the Lydham Heath to Bishop's Castle section, and the town celebrated that night with the ringing of church bells and a bonfire.

When, in October 1865, the branch to Bishop's Castle was completed, it was decided to start services without waiting for either the government inspection of the line or the Montgomery extension. According to Edward Griffith in his booklet *The Bishop's Castle Railway 1865–1935*, passenger services commenced with a locomotive and eleven coaches, probably borrowed from the Mid Wales Railway for the occasion.

Bishop's Castle station had not yet been built but, despite this, large crowds turned out at noon to see the locomotive carrying inscriptions 'Better Late Than Never' and 'Long-Looked-For Come at Last' hauling the coaches laden with shareholders and their friends. In the town, which was decorated with many arches of evergreen, a band played 'See the Conquering Hero Comes' as it headed a long procession. Later about 300 guests sat down to a banquet in a marquee erected on the bowling green adjoining the Castle Hotel. During the evening there was a firework display and the 'navvies' who had built the line were entertained with a meal of roast beef, plum pudding and ale.

Formal opening of the BCR came on 1st February 1866, when regular passenger services began. Initially there were four trains daily in each direction, mostly of a mixed freight and passenger nature. An early 0-4-0ST locomotive named *Bee* had been used during the construction of the line but this was disposed of after

A Bishop's Castle mixed passenger and freight train awaits departure from Lydham Heath in May 1932. (Lens of Sutton)

three years, by which time 0-6-0 *Plowden* had taken its place. The fastest time for the journey was half an hour, although many trains took up to 50 minutes for the 9½ mile trip. Freight provided much of the traffic, particularly on market days at Bishop's Castle, and many wagons were borrowed from the GWR and LMS to supplement the BCR's own meagre fleet.

Passenger traffic remained light throughout the life of the BCR. The station was fairly close to the town centre and no doubt the first regular passenger train of the day awoke many residents, since it left for Craven Arms at 6.10 am. The last daily train returned from Craven Arms at 6.45 pm. In addition, numerous excursions were run, usually associated with local football clubs or events such as the annual Shrewsbury Floral Fete. In order to cater for these, GWR rolling stock was frequently brought in.

Despite financial uncertainty, the BCR still intended to go ahead with the Montgomery and Minsterley lines. However, such hopes were dashed as 1866 progressed, particularly when the Overend & Gurney Bank collapsed causing widespread financial panic throughout the country and affecting many small railways in the course of construction. As a result, the BCR dropped its planned branches, causing investment to slump. By the end of the year, the BCR was close to bankruptcy, and, when creditors could not be satisfied, the law was invoked.

Bailiffs were brought in with one at each terminus and a third accompanied the trains which continued to provide a service. A sale was organised at the George Hotel, Shrewsbury, and many of the company's assets were sold so that creditors could be paid. These included locomotives, goods and passenger vehicles, which together realised £880. Eventually, it was considered that the line could be made to pay and a receiver was appointed to be responsible for the accounts.

All went fairly well for a time, but ten years later, in February 1877, there was another crisis. Legal action was taken against the company by the widow of a director who had sold a parcel of

A mixed train hauled by 0-4-2T no. 1 at Bishop's Castle in the early 1930s. The branch closed completely in 1935. (Lens of Sutton)

74

land for £800 but had never been paid. The High Court agreed an order to pay, and, when this was not settled by the BCR, the railway was duly 'possessed' as from 27th February 1877. An extraordinary state of affairs was to follow.

The lawyers gave notice and, after proceeding to Horderley station, they removed a rail and built a fence across the track, marking the boundary of the property in question. For a time a shuttle service continued between Bishop's Castle and Horderley, from where passengers continued by horse-drawn coaches to Craven Arms. This, however, provided only a temporary solution and it was not long before Bishop's Castle ran very short of coal and other supplies. Desperate measures were needed and a 'council of war' was held in the back parlour of a well known Craven Arms inn.

According to an account in the *Railway Magazine*, a party fortified itself with the cellar's best whisky and later found itself in charge of a shunting engine conveniently heading a number of loaded trucks. Equally conveniently, the signalman in charge

Craven Arms station on the main Shrewsbury–Hereford line. In earlier times trains left for Bishop's Castle or Wellington. (Lens of Sutton)

of the junction, usually closed at night, was still in his cabin. Meantime, two bailiffs guarding the removed section of track were lured to the Red Lion at Horderley where beer tempered with gin proved more comforting than keeping vigil outside on a cold dark night. No sooner had the bailiffs disappeared than a gang of men with lanterns restored the removed rail. The all-clear was given and an engine hauling empties quietly made its way down from Bishop's Castle to Craven Arms, where it picked up the loaded trucks. With a good shove from the LNWR shunting engine, it then steamed as hard as it could for the beleaguered town.

When the bailiffs heard the train coming it was too late for action. They rushed from the Red Lion and waved their lanterns but to no avail. They had been outwitted and despite threats by the lawyers to carry out an arrest, the manager was able to prove an alibi. Although Bishop's Castle had been relieved, the event

Bishop's Castle station after closure. It was felt that had the line been extended to Montgomery as originally planned, it might have proved more successful. (Lens of Sutton)

76

had not solved the BCR's problems, and a meeting was held to discuss reopening the railway.

Various options were talked about, ranging from selling privately, becoming part of the GWR or raising further cash. The last option was adopted even to the extent that a group of local people purchased a locomotive for £700 and then leased it back to the company. On Monday, 2nd July 1877, flags were hung in celebration once again in Bishop's Castle when the line reopened. There were cheers when the first through train left for Craven Arms, and, on its return, church bells were rung and shops were closed for the occasion.

Lydham Heath station was rebuilt around 1906 to consist of a wooden building with two waiting rooms and a small storage shed. It was here that an incident occurred which could have had more serious consequences. At Lydham Heath a reversal was necessary and it was the usual custom for the locomotive to run round the train before going on to Bishop's Castle. Some-

Eaton station in the 1930s. The building survives as a private residence. On reaching Lydham Heath, trains had to reverse for Bishop's Castle. (Lens of Sutton)

times the train was pushed, and there was an occasion when a 'helpful' individual uncoupled the engine on arrival, thinking it would head the train. Unfortunately, this was not so and it was not until the driver applied his brakes as he neared Bishop's Castle that he saw the coaches going on ahead! He whistled furiously to attract the guard's attention, who fortunately stopped the coaches just in time.

Over the ensuing years the line struggled on and several unsuccessful attempts were made to get the GWR to take over the line. By 1931 rumours of closure were rife. A Railway Users' Committee was formed to help the line, but with road traffic successfully competing there was little it could do. Finally it was directed that on 20th April 1935 the line would close completely. Shortly before the end, a train made a journey with just one passenger for the entire journey. During a stop at Eaton, the passenger noted with regret that the timetable posters had been

A recent photograph of Horderley station building. A home signal and a short stretch of restored platform maintain the railway atmosphere. (Author)

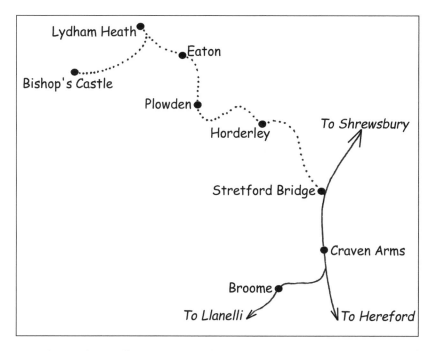

torn from the walls of the waiting room. When this was pointed out to the station-master, back came the reply, 'No, not torn off. The goats have eaten them.'

Today the line is enthusiastically recalled by members of the Bishop's Castle Railway Society. At Horderley the owner of the property has restored a section of platform, a signal has been erected and a station nameplate proudly added. Restoration has been completed on Glenburrel Bridge, the only complete bridge on the old trackbed. Finally, a museum housing numerous fascinating relics and photographs of the BCR in Bishop's Castle is well worth a visit. Despite a disastrous fire in October 2000, it reopened in 2002.

7

Shropshire Quarry Lines

Ludlow/Clee Hill Quarries
Bitterley/Titterstone Quarries
Cleobury Mortimer/Ditton Priors

Ludlow station looking towards Hereford in the 1960s. The station buildings today have gone, replaced by very basic structures. (Lens of Sutton)

Ludlow/Clee Hill Quarries and Bitterley/Titterstone Quarries

A visit to Titterstone Clee Hill can prove a sheer delight. From the top, which stands at 1,750 feet above sea level, there are views over many of the surrounding counties, an attractive spot indeed for the walkers or sightseers who visit the area. Giant

80

golfball-like structures look down, described on the OS map as a satellite earth station. These objects control the paths of aircraft, a far cry indeed from the cranking and groaning railway engines of yesteryear which hauled their various mineral loads up and down the steep hillside.

The Ludlow & Clee Hill Railway, incorporated on 22nd July 1861, was built solely to transport the vast quantities of mineral from Titterstone Clee Hill and Clee Hill. The 4½ mile standard gauge section between Ludlow and Bitterley Yard opened on 24th August 1864, but it was to be another three years before a steep climb from Bitterley to the incline top at the small village of Dhustone began working. The single-track line from Ludlow to Bitterley included a gradient of 1 in 20, enough to strain any locomotive, but with this next section climbing at 1 in 12 and steepening to 1 in 6, it was necessary for loads to be worked by a cable-operated funicular. The line which rose 600 feet in 1¾ miles, included a passing loop, above which tracks converged with a common middle rail to the summit. The system was operated by a stationary steam engine in a winding-drum house situated at the top. The final section to Clee Hill quarries was level by comparison, skirting the south side of the hill and connecting the incline top with a quarry crushing plant. This required a shunting engine permanently based on the hillside section.

In addition to the Clee Hill quarries line, another short stretch climbed from Bitterley Yard to Titterstone quarry on nearby

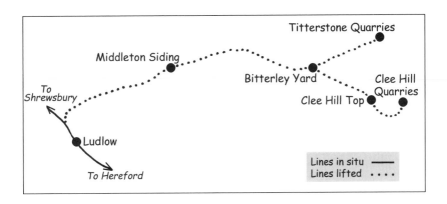

The remains of the trackbed at Clee Hill Top, where trains were hauled by wire rope up a gradient steepening to 1 in 6. (Author)

Titterstone Clee Hill. This was a 3ft-gauge self-acting rail system, privately owned by British Quarrying Co Ltd, with the full trucks going down providing the momentum for those going up. This incline closed in 1952, but, visiting the area today, it is possible to find where the incline crossed above the village of Bedlam (or Titterstone as it is now called). Abutments are still in existence just beyond Titterstone Cottages.

Minerals were lowered from the top of the Clee Hill quarries standard gauge incline by four wagons plus a brake truck at a speed of not more than 6 mph. The maximum load permitted per wagon was 85 tons. On the Ludlow to Bitterley stretch there were problems when the rails were wet or slippery, and it was not unusual for the tank locomotives coming from Ludlow to rush the gradient or even halve their loads. A water tower built at the foot of the gradient often proved necessary for drivers when the engines were struggling.

In 1893 the Ludlow & Clee Hill Railway was taken over by the

GWR 0-6-0PT no. 29 waits with coaches in a siding at Cleobury Mortimer station in 1935. The line played an important role during the Second World War, when ammunition was stored in the area. (John H. Meredith)

Shrewsbury & Hereford (LNWR & GWR Joint) Railway. Business remained brisk and by the end of the First World War the delivery of stone was even busier. There were times when around 6,000 tons of stone were being despatched from the quarries each week. By the 1930s, as roads improved, competition from lorries caused the rail traffic to fall away. Despite this, the branch remained active for some time. During its last years, various LMS/GWR (later BR) locomotives worked the line. Four wheeled Sentinel engines (built 1928/1930) were a frequent sight, as were two South Wales 0-4-0 saddle tanks, formerly with the Swansea Harbour Trust Railway as GWR 1142 and 1143. It was in fact 1143 that was the last to work at Clee Hill prior to closure of the incline on 7th November 1960. Over two years later, on 31st December 1962, the line from Ludlow (Clee Hill junction) to Bitterley Yard closed officially.

Cleobury Mortimer/Ditton Priors

As far as passengers were concerned, the Cleobury Mortimer & Ditton Priors Light Railway (CM&DPLR) lasted only 30 years. Although the last regular passenger train travelled the line on 26th September 1938, another 27 years were to pass before the line closed completely.

An Act agreeing a light railway from Cleobury Mortimer to Ditton Priors was granted on 23rd March 1901; yet it took some seven years before the 12½ mile line could open. There were financial problems and it was not until March 1906 that a tender was accepted. On 23rd January 1907 the first sod was cut, although without any ceremony. Work commenced two days later, and in June 1907 a connection was made with the GWR line at Cleobury Mortimer. The line opened to freight traffic on 19th July 1908 and a daily goods train, initially hauled by contractors' locomotives, was possible. Passenger services commenced on

Ditton Priors station soon after its opening in 1908 with Brown Clee Hill in the background. The branch of nearly 12 miles opened to provide a rail outlet for quarried stone. (Lens of Sutton)

84

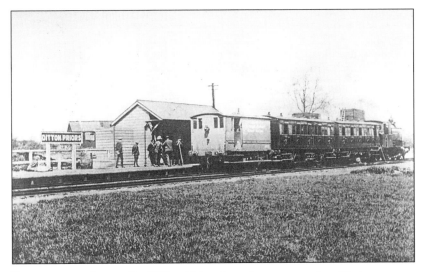

Passenger services on the Ditton Priors branch commenced on 21st November 1908 when two mixed trains ran on certain weekdays only. Picture taken at Ditton Priors terminus. (Lens of Sutton)

21st November 1908 after a Board of Trade inspection of the line had been completed. At first two mixed trains ran each way on certain weekdays only. Manning Wardle 0-6-0ST locomotives 1734 and 1735, named *Burwarton*, after Lord Boyne's estate, and *Cleobury*, were available together with four four-wheeled oil-lit coaches. The latter were purchased from Bow Works in London and were conversions from North London Railway coaches.

The line was built principally to provide a rail outlet for stone quarried on the adjacent Clee Hills. Much of the stone came from the Clee Hill Granite Company's Magpie Quarries on Titterstone Clee Hill and it was carried by means of a 3½ mile aerial ropeway, which reached the railway at Detton Ford Siding. Another quarry on Brown Clee Hill (1,792 ft) was operated by the Abdon Clee Stone Quarrying Company. Here stone was brought down a rope-worked incline to connect with a siding at Ditton Priors. There was a considerable demand for the stone, particularly in growing urban areas where, prior to 1914, it was used to produce 6 ins by 9 ins tramway setts.

0-6-0PT Burwarton no. 28 with mixed passenger and goods awaits departure at Cleobury Mortimer station. Coaches were four-wheeled throughout the branch's existence. (Lens of Sutton)

The CM&DPLR began its life with great hopes for the future. Freight from the quarries generated considerable business, with both the GWR and the Midland Railway bringing in their wagons. Occasionally, passenger trains connected with Kidderminster, where the market was popular, and in August 1909 many travelled by rail to attend an industrial, horticultural and poultry show at Burwarton. On that occasion the line's capacity was stretched to its maximum when 300 extra passengers were catered for in one day. In 1910 some 15,000 passengers and 77,000 tons of freight were carried and in 1911 the operating surplus almost doubled.

Because of the surge in popularity, consideration was given to extending beyond the existing branch. Proposals for a Stottesdon, Kinlet and Billingsley light railway as a means to bring coal from collieries both at Billingsley and Kinlet to join the CM&DPLR at Stottesdon came to nothing. Coal from the Billingsley colliery was eventually carried by mineral line to join the Severn Valley Railway between Highley and Arley. There was also speculation that the line might extend beyond Ditton Priors to Presthope to join the Craven Arms/Buildwas line or the Severn Valley branch at either Bridgnorth or Coalport but again nothing happened.

In the couple of years leading up to the First World War passenger traffic fell disappointingly, a situation hardly surprising in such a rural area. Yet soon after hostilities had begun in 1914 freight traffic improved considerably. Stone from the quarries found new customers and quantities were railed regularly to Aldershot. Wagons were soon in short supply and many more were acquired. The GWR lent class 850 0-6-0PT locomotive no. 2001 to the CM&DPLR for a time to help out. As the war progressed, freight traffic in timber also increased.

The wartime period also saw the development of prefabricated buildings at the Abdon Clee Stone Quarry. Sections were made using the right mix of cement and stone and it was intended the system should be adapted to many types of construction. A number of local buildings were erected in this way, including a new village hall at Ditton Priors. The railway company's offices at Cleobury Town were also prefabricated.

After the war, in 1919, the two locomotives, having now served over 10 years' faithful duty, took turns to go away to Worcester for repairs. In the same year peace celebrations took place and to mark the event the Abdon Clee Quarry managing director treated his employees and all in the parish to a lavish tea. On 19th August 1921 the Railways Act became law, this requiring the railways of Great Britain to be merged into four groups. In consequence, the CM&DPLR on 25th May 1922 became part of the Great Western Railway.

The locomotives 1734 *Burwarton* and 1735 *Cleobury* therefore became GWR stock but they were renumbered 28 and 29. The GWR decided that they justified an extensive rebuild, so in 1930 they were both sent to Swindon. During their absence, 8650 class 0-6-0ST no. 1948 and 0-6-0ST no. 1970 were delivered from Kidderminster to keep the branch going. Both *Burwarton* and *Cleobury* were eventually returned to the branch rebuilt as pannier tank locomotives. Early in 1926 the four North London

Burwarton station in earlier times. It was little used and it became a halt in 1923. The station was in fact closer to the village of Charlcotte than Burwarton. (Lens of Sutton)

Railway coaches were withdrawn and in their place came GWR gas-lit four-wheeled coaches.

Passenger traffic continued to decline. In a GWR timetable of the 1920s it was pointed out that stops would only be made at some stations 'if required'. By the early 1930s the quantities of stone carried had dropped considerably and traffic along the line was reduced to two mixed trains daily. Closure to passenger traffic became inevitable and soon closure notices were displayed. Even so, petitions were organised to keep the line working but these had no effect. When the last passenger train ran on Saturday, 24th September 1938, so many people turned up that two extra four-wheeled carriages had to be added to the two already in use.

Yet as the passenger traffic ceased, so freight traffic received a dramatic boost. As a result of the 1938 Munich crisis, arms were being produced and the CM&DPLR area was considered safe for ammunition storage. Nissen huts were built along the line in readiness, and, when hostilities began in September 1939, no. 29 was sent to Worcester Works so that a spark arresting cowl could be fitted to her chimney. At first this was to protect ammunition vans from occasional sparks thrown out from the locomotive when tackling a gradient but later it was needed as a protection when working in the armament depot. The area was subsequently selected by the Admiralty as a naval armament depot.

The one-time quiet branch was now a place of activity, with the depot assuming strategic importance. Sturdy locomotives were brought in to handle the heavy loads over the numerous steep gradients. In their informative book *The Cleobury Mortimer and Ditton Priors Light Railway*, W. Smith and K. Beddoes wrote that the depot even got a mention from the German wartime propagandist 'Lord Haw Haw'. Searchlights were installed at several places along the route and decoy fires were set up on the nearby Clee Hills. Happily the depot remained intact throughout the war, the nearest bombs being dropped near Cleobury town (at Walltown Farm).

After peace returned in 1945 the line gradually ran down again. Nationalisation came in 1948 with the line incorporated into BR's Western Region. No great changes were made except that no. 29 had a new cowl fitted and no. 28, after a short stay on loan at Hereford, returned via Worcester with a new chimney. No. 28 later had a spell shunting at NCB Hafod Colliery at Wrexham. Meantime, freight traffic along the CM&DPLR branch continued at a fairly leisurely pace with sometimes only one journey per week.

Some 17 years after closure to passengers, 21st May 1955 proved to be a day of some significance for the branch when a Stephenson Locomotive Society train ran from Birmingham via Kidderminster and Bewdley to Ditton Priors. The four-coach train arrived at Cleobury Mortimer hauled by Dean 0-6-0 no. 2516 (later preserved at Swindon), where 0-6-0PT class 2021 no. 2144, fitted with spark arrestor, took over. The train, the first passenger bogie-stock ever to cover the line, travelled as far as Cleobury North sidings before returning.

In May 1957 the Admiralty took over ownership of the line and five months later it was responsible for operation, with two Ruston and Hornsby 0-4-0 diesel shunters providing the occasional haulage power. In August 1962 the line between

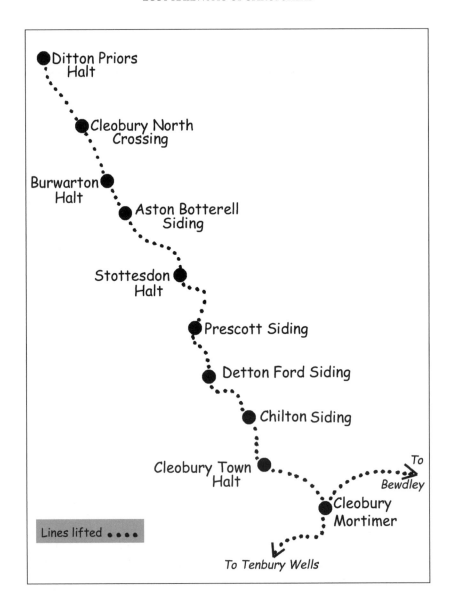

Bewdley and Tenbury Wells closed to passenger traffic and closure of the Ditton Priors branch by the Admiralty seemed inevitable. Eventually, all traffic ceased on Good Friday, 16th April 1965, the same day the line from Cleobury Mortimer to Bewdley also completely closed.

Lifting of the track was delayed by removal of Admiralty equipment by rail from the depot. When track demolition began in earnest later in the year, suggestions were made that the line should be preserved but the difficulties appeared too great and the idea was dropped. Two years later, local residents were surprised to read in their newspapers about a report in the House of Commons that the line might be 'reopened to serve a new American army base at Ditton Priors'. The Americans may have moved in but the railway had already gone! Many of the rails and sleepers had been taken up and some of the land had been sold. The Americans stayed at the depot for only 18 months.

Ditton Priors station area is a trading estate today. The water towers used by the railway are still there, and also numerous buildings that housed naval personnel. (Author)

Recollections of railway days remain at the former Cleobury Mortimer
station building, today, private residences, with doors carrying name plates
from the past. (Author)

When visiting in 2001, the author found numerous relics to recall the earlier days. At Ditton Priors, the former terminus and today a trading estate, two water tanks remain in situ adjacent to the former platform, and nearby stands a row of railway cottages. Many of the buildings on the estate remain as reminders of the time when naval personnel were billeted in the area. Travelling the branch southwards there was very little to be found. The numerous wooden built halts had long since disappeared. Just off the B4363 the prefabricated Cleobury Town station concrete railway office, built in 1917, was still there as a private residence. An old buffer stop helped form part of an end wall to a nearby garden shed.

The station building and platform edge at Cleobury Mortimer (near the Blount Arms) have survived. For many years after closure, the station's nameboard stood amongst the weeds stating 'Cleobury Mortimer. Change for Ditton Priors Railway'.

A close-up of a sign on the wall of the former Cleobury Mortimer station building. The station closed in August 1962 to passenger traffic but continued to serve goods traffic between Cleobury Mortimer and Bewdley until April 1965. (Author)

A short distance away there was a bridge which carried the branch over the Bewdley-Cleobury Mortimer road. After final closure of the line the army was called in to blow it up. According to local legend, a pot of gold sovereigns had been bricked in when the bridge was built, yet no trace was found. When the author visited the remains of the abutments in 2003 he had a poke around in the undergrowth – just in case.

8

Along Shropshire's Border

Woofferton/Tenbury Wells/Bewdley

GWR Churchward class 4500 2-6-2T no. 4596 waits at Woofferton station probably in the late 1940s. The station closed to passengers in July 1961. (Lens of Sutton)

The Kington, Leominster and Stourport Canal was an ambitious project intended to open up a route to the river Severn as well as the industrial Midlands. Three large aqueducts, four tunnels (with one over 2 miles in length) and some 16 locks were planned, although in the event only a stretch of some 18 miles of continuous waterway, from Leominster to just beyond Newnham, was completed. The section cost £93,000 to build but it did not prove successful and no dividend was ever paid to shareholders.

Two miles from Newnham, close to the A456, the 1,250 yd long Southnet tunnel was built. It was completed in 1795 but it collapsed in the same year, and, according to local rumours, two men and a boat are still entombed there! It was proposed that the remainder of the journey to Stourport should be completed by tramway but this did not come about. What existed of the canal struggled through the first half of the 19th century to be eventually sold to the Shrewsbury & Hereford Railway (S&HR). The canal closed for good in 1859 and in the same year the Tenbury Railway Company (helped by the S&HR) was incorporated.

The single-track railway between Woofferton and Bewdley crossed the county boundaries of Worcestershire, Shropshire and Herefordshire several times during its run through attractive and unspoilt countryside. The first section between Woofferton and Tenbury Wells opened on 1st August 1861 and was worked by the GWR. Tenbury Wells remained a terminus for only three years, after which time the Tenbury & Bewdley Railway, incorporated in 1860, completed the section to Bewdley. This was also GWR worked and it opened on 13th August 1864.

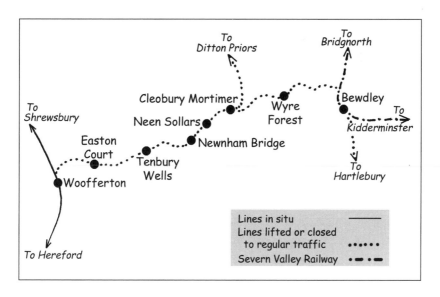

Two companies now existed but the lines were soon integrated into one long branch, although certain trains did continue to run between Woofferton and Tenbury Wells only. In June 1878 a three mile link between Bewdley and Kidderminster opened, which meant that through trains were possible not only from Woofferton to Kidderminster but also for a time there were through connections between Woofferton and Birmingham and Wolverhampton.

According to a letter published in *Railway Magazine* in the 1930s, there was once a time when the name Woofferton was spelt correctly on the nameboards, yet on the signal box it read 'Wofferton' and the platform trolleys displayed 'Wooferton'! Leaving Woofferton station, the branch bore sharply eastwards along the Teme valley, stretches of it being built along the abandoned Leominster Canal.

The first intermediate station was Easton Court, which was known as 'Easton Court for Little Hereford'. Easton Court station closed to passengers only a year after opening but

Easton Court station between Woofferton and Tenbury Wells seen here after closure. The station building is a private residence today. (Lens of Sutton)

reopened three years later in April 1865. Despite the sparsely populated locality, Station House was a substantial building and this has survived today as a private dwelling. There was once an aqueduct at Little Hereford which carried the Leominster Canal over the river Teme but, much to the annoyance of the local folk, this was blown up during the Second World War, presumably to prevent its use by possible invaders!

By the 1840s, Tenbury Wells had become established as a small spa, following the discovery of saline springs in the area. Tenbury Wells station was in fact situated in Burford, which was about half a mile from Tenbury Wells. Burford was the seat of Lord Northwick, who with a number of local landowners had done much to get a railway into the area. Tenbury Wells station had two platforms, a number of goods sidings and, in its early years, a turntable. For a time it had two signal boxes but its West box closed in the 1920s. The station was initially known as just Tenbury but in 1912 it was renamed Tenbury Wells.

Locomotive 0-4-2T No. 1445 hauls an auto train at Tenbury Wells on 7th October 1960. After complete closure in 1964, the station was demolished to become an industrial estate. (D.K. Jones Collection)

In the early 1920s the branch saw five trains each way daily (none on Sundays) between Kidderminster and Woofferton, although a further five made the daily 12 minute journey between Tenbury Wells and Woofferton. Various tank and tender locomotives were used on the line, and, when traffic was sparse, it was not unusual to see an engine hauling a single carriage. In later years GWR diesel railcars were used for many of the passenger services. During the Second World War there was an increase in traffic when considerable quantities of ammunition were carried to and from the Cleobury Mortimer to Ditton Priors branch line.

After the war traffic suffered from road competition, yet a proposal from British Rail on 31st July 1961 to close the entire line to passengers was strongly resisted. Closure of Woofferton station and the withdrawal of all traffic between Woofferton and Tenbury Wells went ahead and Woofferton station was subsequently demolished. Passenger services between Tenbury

Tenbury Wells station opened in August 1861 as a terminus for trains from Woofferton. Three years later a line reached Tenbury Wells from Bewdley. Both were GWR worked. (Lens of Sutton)

Wells and Bewdley continued but were reduced to only a weekday morning train and a return train in the evening. This service survived only a year, ending on 1st August 1962. Goods services lasted a further two years, terminating between Tenbury Wells and Cleobury Mortimer in January 1964, with the final stretch between Cleobury Mortimer and Bewdley ending early in 1965. After closure, Tenbury Wells station was totally demolished and the site was developed as an industrial estate, although a road bridge still exists.

Enter a shop just up a short drive off the A456 at Newnham Bridge and you are in what was once the station building. Outside, part of the station yard has become a garden centre. The platform and building remain intact but the station nameboard has been copied. To add further realism there is a signal and a truck at the end of the platform both of which were acquired

Newnham Bridge, an intermediary station on the Tenbury Wells–Bewdley line, photographed June 2001, some 38 years after closure. The station has been preserved as part of the Station House Nursery. (Author)

from the Birmingham area. Originally the station had a signal box but it was later replaced by three ground frames. The single platform was so sited that access from the road had to be made over the track and it was necessary for strict instructions to be issued to avoid the possibility of vehicles obstructing the running line. At times Newnham Bridge proved a busy station, particularly when fruit was in season.

Beyond, in a very isolated area, followed Neen Sollars, a minor station which, after closure, survived as a private dwelling. Next came Cleobury Mortimer, sited about a mile and a half east of the town. Here the track layout was altered when the Cleobury Mortimer and Ditton Priors Light Railway opened in 1908 (see Chapter 7). The remains of Cleobury Mortimer station can be found up a short drive by the Blount Arms, just to the south of the A4117. The station building is today private flats

Neen Sollers former station building between Tenbury Wells and Cleobury Mortimer can still be found in an isolated area near the small village. The station closed completely in 1964. When visited in June 2001, work to restore the building was in hand. (Author)

Cleobury Mortimer, between Tenbury Wells and Bewdley, also served as a junction to the Cleobury Mortimer & Ditton Priors Light Railway. The station was about 1½ miles to the east of the town, which meant that many passengers had to face a long, hilly walk. (Lens of Sutton)

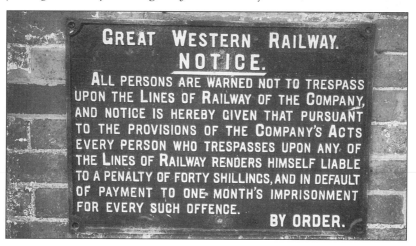

GREAT WESTERN RAILWAY.
NOTICE.
ALL PERSONS ARE WARNED NOT TO TRESPASS UPON THE LINES OF RAILWAY OF THE COMPANY, AND NOTICE IS HEREBY GIVEN THAT PURSUANT TO THE PROVISIONS OF THE COMPANY'S ACTS EVERY PERSON WHO TRESPASSES UPON ANY OF THE LINES OF RAILWAY RENDERS HIMSELF LIABLE TO A PENALTY OF FORTY SHILLINGS, AND IN DEFAULT OF PAYMENT TO ONE MONTH'S IMPRISONMENT FOR EVERY SUCH OFFENCE.
BY ORDER.

A reminder of GWR days on the wall of the preserved Newnham Bridge station building. During its heyday this was a busy station particularly when fruit was in season. (Author)

and notices on the wall and doorways recall when trains once called.

The last intermediate station before meeting the SVR at Bewdley was Wyre Forest, where much of the track wound its way through heavily graded curves. This small and no doubt little-used station closed with the line in 1962, and today, difficult to find on a minor road, the station building and platform have survived as an attractive private residence. Outside, by the roadway, can be seen a discarded sleeper with a chair in situ and along the platform a concrete post that once supported fencing now proudly carries a bird box.

Between Wyre Forest station and Bewdley the trackbed passes through the Wyre Forest Nature Reserve. Striking out from the visitor centre, which is located on the A456 two miles west of Bewdley, several designated walks can be taken where the forestry blends splendidly with the wildlife and where much of the area is also a Site of Special Scientific Interest. Walking on a little further the trackbed can be found as it winds through the forest alongside Dowles Brook. This leads towards where the three-span Dowles viaduct once carried trains over the river Severn to join the track of the SVR and continue to Bewdley.

9

The Severn Valley Railway and a Line Restored

Shrewsbury/Bridgnorth/Bewdley/Hartlebury
Bridgnorth/Bewdley/Kidderminster Town

GWR 0-6-0 no. 2516 stands in Shrewsbury's station awaiting departure.
Services on the original Severn Valley Railway began in February 1862.
(Lens of Sutton)

Shrewsbury/Bridgnorth/Bewdley/ Hartlebury

Passengers stood contentedly at Highley station waiting for a Kidderminster train. The attractive location and stone building had changed little over the years since the station first opened to the public on 1st February 1862. Carefully tended flower gardens enhanced the area, and GWR notices gave train times. Nearby an advertisement read 'Craven A will not affect your throat' and at the end of the platform a notice threatened. 'Shut the gate: The Penalty is FIFTY POUNDS for leaving this gate unlocked.'

It was not long before LMS locomotive 4-6-0 class 5 no. 45110, known as *Black Five*, steamed round the single-track bend into the station, hauling numerous chocolate and cream coloured GWR coaches. Soon passengers alighted, others clambered aboard, a whistle blew and the train continued its journey to Kidderminster. Yet this was not the 1950s or even earlier – the date was Saturday, 1st November 2003 and it was of course a visit to the ever popular present-day Severn Valley Railway (SVR).

Parliament agreed as early as 1853 that the original Severn Valley Railway could be built but it was to be another nine years before the line came into being. When completed, it provided a link between the county towns of Worcestershire and Shropshire. It also made possible rail transport to a number of industrial and agricultural areas. Regular services between Shrewsbury and Hartlebury via Stourport began on 1st February 1862 and they were worked by the West Midland Railway (WMR).

The formal opening had taken place on the previous day, when a special train of 22 coaches had left Worcester Shrub Hill bound for Shrewsbury. The passengers included the chairman of the GWR, the chairman of the SVR and the general manager of the WMR. At Shrewsbury three more coaches and an extra locomotive were added, after which the train returned non-stop to Bridgnorth where the passengers enjoyed a public dinner at the assembly room, followed by various speeches.

The line of almost 40 miles was single throughout, and, although it followed the course of the river Severn, fairly steep gradients were necessary, reaching 1 in 100 in places. Numerous viaducts had been required, and tunnels included one of 594 yds at Bridgnorth to take the tracks under the town and another, 480 yds long, between Bewdley and Stourport. Along the line there

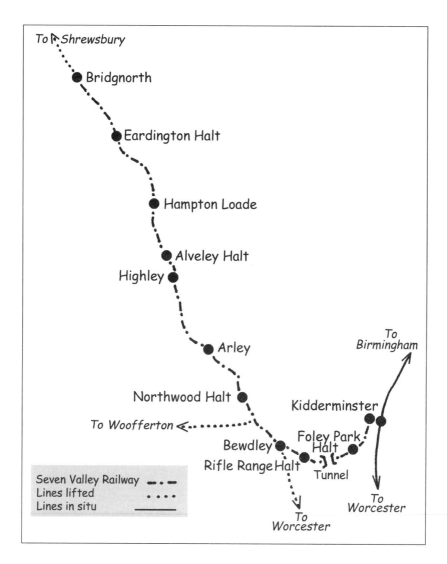

were 13 intermediate stations. Most of these had two platforms and a loop, although a number began their existence with just one platform and no loop.

The SVR provided four passenger trains each way daily

A stiff penalty for not shutting the gate at the end of Highley platform! (Author)

between Shrewsbury and Bridgnorth with further services available south to Hartlebury. There were useful amounts of freight, much of it agricultural or coal traffic coming from the Highley area. To the north there were links at Buildwas with the market town of Much Wenlock and on to Craven Arms on the Shrewsbury & Hereford Railway. Buildwas became a busy junction, with its platforms at two levels, and the stationmaster had a staff of ten.

On 18th July 1872 the SVR was absorbed into the GWR, which in 1878 opened a link between Kidderminster and Bewdley. This meant that trains from Birmingham and the West Midlands could reach the Severn Valley. Bewdley became a crossing point, with many Hartlebury trains running northwards to Bridgnorth, while many Kidderminster trains continued to run to Woofferton via Tenbury.

Throughout its life the SVR was never financially successful, although freight made a useful contribution. Agricultural and

Hartlebury when it served as a junction for Severn Valley line trains to Shrewsbury. Note the tall chimney on the right of the picture. (Lens of Sutton)

Hartlebury station, between Worcester and Kidderminster, July 2002. The station awning and the footbridge have gone, but the nearby signal box has survived and the tall chimney on the right is still there. (Author)

107

Ironbridge & Broseley probably taken in the 1950s. GWR 5100 class 2-6-2T locomotive no. 5153 hauls numerous freight wagons. The station closed completely in 1963. (Lens of Sutton)

coal traffic from the Highley area was one of the SVR's principal sources of income. By the 1930s, despite increasing competition from the motor car, five trains were running daily from Hartlebury or Kidderminster to Shrewsbury, with additional auto-trains covering the stretch to Bridgnorth. As the number of passengers diminished, halts were opened in the hope of attracting further business. Many of the earlier tender loco-motives had now gone and passenger trains were hauled by class 4500 2-6-2Ts. Diesel railcars were also making an appearance. Coal from Alveley Colliery, north of Highley, was generally hauled by class 4300 2-6-0 locomotives.

Towards the end of the line's life there was a strange occurrence. According to W. B. Herbert in his book *Railway Ghosts*, a Mr Reynolds saw himself in a premonition standing on the footplate of class 4MT 2-6-0 43106, leaving Bridgnorth smokebox and heading for Bewdley. As the cab crossed the bridge the first full-span cross-beam collapsed onto a green Morris Minor passing underneath and the engine fell onto the road below. After a subsequent similar premonition, Mr Reynolds related the incidents to his wife. When a further person had a similar premonition, it was decided something should be done.

On examination the suspect bridge was found to have a number of loose rivets as well as serious corrosion affecting one side of the first three cross-beams. The situation was reported and the chief civil engineer imposed a strict speed limit on the bridge. Three months later a new bridge was fitted but Mr Reynolds had further experiences. On one occasion he and his wife saw the vague aura of a human form on the firebox top of no. 43106 and both sensed impending danger. They called the apparition Arnold and concluded that he was a ghost who liked railway engines and who would appear from time to time to warn of impending accidents!

The Second World War brought renewed activity to the SVR, with a large RAF camp near Bridgnorth. After the war, traffic dwindled again and neighbouring lines were facing closure. To

Cound Halt, between Berrington and Cressage, opened on 4th August 1934 to encourage traffic. It was sited close to a ferry which crossed the River Severn. (Lens of Sutton)

the north, the Much Wenlock to Craven Arms section closed to passengers on 31st December 1951 and ten years later, on 31st July 1961, the Woofferton to Tenbury stretch closed. Passenger services between Bewdley and Tenbury survived only until 1962, the same year that the line from Much Wenlock to Buildwas and Wellington closed. It was already very clear that the SVR Shrewsbury to Hartlebury route was under threat.

The entire line from Shrewsbury to Bewdley closed on 9th September 1963. It was a sad day for many when the last regular passenger train left Bridgnorth for Shrewsbury at 7.27 pm on Saturday, 7th September 1963, hauled by class 2 locomotive 2-6-2T no. 41207. A coal service between Buildwas and Alveley Colliery Sidings (approximately 1½ miles north of Highley station) closed on 30th November 1963, and when the stretch between Alveley Sidings and Bewdley closed 3rd February 1969 the colliery's rail link had come to a complete end.

All that was left for passengers was a Kidderminster/Bewdley/Stourport/Hartlebury shuttle. There were strong protests when closure of these lines was announced and a date planned for 7th April 1969 had to be postponed. Eventually, when, at 7.20 pm on Saturday, 3rd January 1970, the last train left Bewdley for Kidderminster, it seemed that passenger traffic along any part of the attractive Severn Valley had truly come to an end. Yet this was far from the case. Efforts to restore steam along the SVR had already been in hand for a number of years.

Bridgnorth/Bewdley/Kidderminster Town

The Severn Valley Railway Society was formed on 6th July 1965, when a group of enthusiasts met at Kidderminster. North of Bridgnorth, station track had been lifted, but between Alveley Sidings and Bewdley BR had continued to operated coal trains. The society's intention was to run passenger trains from Bridgnorth to Hampton Loade (just over 4 miles), and after two weeks of negotiation a price of £25,000 was agreed, with BR to cover all freehold land, buildings and track. A deposit of 10% was paid the following year and within a further three years,

A southbound GWR Collett 2-6-2T locomotive with passenger coaches arrives at Bewdley in the late 1930s. In 1878 a link line was built between Bewdley and Kidderminster, which meant trains from Shrewsbury could run directly to and from the Birmingham area. (Lens of Sutton)

after considerable fund raising, the remainder was paid.

There was great excitement when, on Saturday, 23rd May 1970, the first public passenger train left Bridgnorth. Six GWR coaches were hauled by 2251 class ex-GWR locomotive no. 3205 to Hampton Loade and back; with an hourly service following. Earlier in 1969 Alveley Colliery had closed and SVR members' eyes were already looking further southwards. With Bewdley closed by BR to passengers in January 1970, the way seemed clear to press through Bewdley to Foley Park, near Kidderminster. A further campaign followed, ably assisted by the late Sir Gerald Nabarro, MP for Worcester South since 1961 and also a rail enthusiast. The target of £110,000 was reached and £74,000 was spent on purchasing the railway to Foley Park.

After a tremendous effort by Severn Valley engineering volunteers, Highley was reached in April 1974 with Bewdley following one month later. The final goal of reaching

Passengers wait at Bewdley for a north-bound train. Regular Severn Valley Railway services first re-commenced between Bridgnorth and Bewdley on 18th May 1974. (Author)

The first SVR train reached Kidderminster on 30th July 1984, and regular services began during December. Ex-LMS 2-8-0 locomotive class 8F no. 8233 (photographed at Kidderminster in 1989) has quite a history. Built in 1940, it served in France and later spent time in Iran and then Egypt. It is now renumbered 48773. (Author)

GWR locomotive 4-6-0 Raveningham Hall *photographed at Bridgnorth on 1st August 1977. The locomotive is kept at the Gloucester Warwickshire Railway. (D.K. Jones Collection)*

Kidderminster seemed within the SVR's reach but further obstacles had to be overcome. The 2-mile section from Bewdley to Foley Park, although purchased by the SVR in 1974, had been used only on special occasions, such as steam events for enthusiasts. Sugar factory traffic between Foley Park and Kidderminster ceased in 1982 but the line remained available to link BR with the SVR. Eyes turned once again to Kidderminster but problems persisted. BR traffic between Stourbridge and Worcester (via Kidderminster) had become so poor that closure of the section was considered. Happily for the SVR the line was saved when local services between Gloucester and Birmingham were routed via Kidderminster instead of Bromsgrove, the latter stretch being needed for new high speed trains from May 1983.

During 1983/4 over £370,000 was raised by share issue and out of this £75,000 went on the purchase of the stretch of line between Foley Park and Kidderminster. The balance was to be

The 11.45 am train from Kidderminster to Bewdley prepares to leave, 27th June 2001, hauled by GWR locomotive no. 5764 class 5700 0-6-0PT built in 1929. (Author)

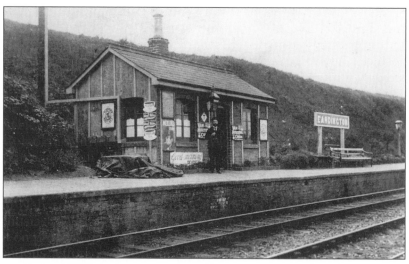

Eardington Halt in earlier SVR days when it served as a useful stopping place with watering facilities. (Lens of Sutton)

used to develop the former BR goods yard site at Comberton Hill to form a new SVR Kidderminster Town station. Finally, on 30th July 1984, the great day came. The first train to enter Kidderminster was a VIP special, headed by 4-6-0 no. 4930 *Hagley Hall*.

Work to construct Kidderminster Town station buildings began later in 1984 thanks to a grant of £60,000 from the English Tourist Board. It was completed in stages and was officially opened to the public by Michael Spicer, MP, Parliamentary Secretary of State for Transport, on 4th July 1986. The popularity of the new station was undoubted. Situated close to the BR station, the number of passengers using the SVR reached over 190,000 in the first full year at Kidderminster.

Today the Severn Valley Railway continues in popularity, bringing pleasure to the many thousands of visitors who travel the line throughout most of the year. With its many enthusiastic supporters, it is worth recalling that the Severn Valley Railway has the largest collection of locomotives and rolling stock in the UK. A couple of years ago the SVR celebrated its 30th anniversary. It has come a long way since its modest beginnings in May 1970, when public services first ran between Bridgnorth and Hampton Loade.

10

A Line to Stafford and Rivals across the Severn

Wellington/Newport/Stafford
Wellington/Oakengates/Coalport (East)

In the 1950s scores of steam trains stopped at Wellington. Ex LMS 2-6-2T hauls the 1.02 pm train from Crewe on the 12th August 1963. (D.K. Jones Collection)

Wellington/Newport/Stafford

There was a day in 1852 that villagers of Donnington, just to the north of Telford, would have long remembered. The trouble began at Shrewsbury when, on 29th July, a train from Stafford arrived with the driver complaining that the LNWR *Mazeppa*

116

no. 24, a 2-2-2 locomotive of Trevithic-Allan design built at Crewe in 1849, had problems. The foreman instructed the night cleaner, Thompson, to deal with it, but early next morning when the driver arrived to prepare the engine he found it was missing. Thompson had earlier fired *Mazeppa* but had left the engine in forward gear with the regulator open.

It was soon realised that the locomotive with no one aboard was steaming towards Stafford. There was an immediate hue and cry, and an available engine was sent in hot pursuit. The driver soon saw flying steam in the distance but he could do nothing. It was not until Donnington that the runaway engine came to an unfortunate stop, crashing into the back of an early train bound for Stafford and killing one of the few passengers. Thompson was woken from his sleep at Shrewsbury to find himself facing a charge of manslaughter.

The line from Wellington to Stafford began its life by an Act of Parliament dated 3rd August 1846 and submitted by the Shropshire Union Railways & Canal Company (SUR&CC). The

Days at Wellington, long since gone, when the station had a bookstall and milk travelled by rail. (Lens of Sutton)

company was soon to become a pawn in the battles between the LNWR and the GWR to reach the Mersey. Less than a year later the SUR&CC was leased to the LNWR.

Earlier there had been numerous ambitious plans put forward by the SUR&CC, many of these comprising lines to be built along the banks of bankrupted canals. Such routes included a branch from Stafford to Stone in the Potteries plus another between Crewe and Newtown in Wales. Canal owners had been forced to gradually give way to railway schemes, as the railways proved themselves superior, and the canal company's plans to build further long stretches of canals never materialised.

The Wellington to Stafford line opened on 1st June 1849, the same day that services commenced between Shrewsbury and Oakengates. Most people welcomed the trains, which provided new links with the rest of the country, and it was expected that the agricultural and industrial trades would greatly benefit. The line from Stafford to Wellington was 18½ miles in length and for

Earlier days at Wellington (today known as Wellington Telford West) when trains went direct to Stafford. The branch closed to passenger traffic in 1964. (Lens of Sutton)

a time it had the advantage that it was the only link between Shrewsbury and London. By taking a train to Stafford, passengers could continue on the LNWR to Euston. Three trains daily connected with London trains and this was doubled within a year or so. However, fares were not cheap, for the second class cost to travel from Shrewsbury to Stafford was 3s 10d and the fare to London (also second class) was £1, a figure well above the average weekly wage. Third class or 'Parliamentary' trains were available but these generally left Shrewsbury between 3 am and 5 am in the morning, which to most was quite unacceptable.

Meantime, the Shrewsbury & Birmingham Railway (S&BR) was struggling to reach Birmingham. Wet weather held up work on large embankments at Shifnal and also work in Oakengates tunnel. There was further aggravation when Sunday working was introduced, with clerics complaining it was a 'flagrant violation of the Sabbath'. It was to be another five years before Birmingham was reached, but, when completed, it meant that passengers could travel 30 miles directly from Shrewsbury to Birmingham instead of 46 miles via Stafford. A bitter price war began, and, after massive reductions by the SUR&CC, the price dropped to as little as one penny for ten miles. People were quick to take advantage and trains into Shrewsbury from around Newport and Wellington were often carrying over a thousand passengers each!

After leaving the S&BR line, the first intermediate station from Wellington to Stafford was Hadley. As a village Hadley dates back to Saxon times and has numerous claims to fame. Hadley Park Mill, powered by both water and steam, was probably the only such mill of its kind in Shropshire, and a lock at Hadley Park was last used in the 1930s. During the 18th century Hadley Park Hall was occupied by the celebrated ironmaster John Wilkinson.

After Trench Crossing and Donnington, the next station was Newport. Although a village, this was the only intermediate station of any significance, for in later years few passengers used the service beyond to Stafford. Today much of the former trackbed has gone and Newport station has been completely

119

Trench Crossing station on the line from Wellington to Stafford. An LMS Fowler locomotive 2-6-4T hauls a passenger train in 1957. Trench Crossing station closed in September 1964. (Russell Mulford)

This was all that is left of Trench Crossing station in May 1992. The picture, taken looking towards Hadley, shows the remains of the platform for Stafford-bound trains. If planners succeed, this line could reopen at a future date to connect Wellington with an MOD depot at Donnington. (Russell Mulford)

demolished to make way for a housing estate. Passing through Newport on the A41, it is possible to see a redundant road bridge to the east across a field. There is yet another reminder of Newport at the Blists Hill Open Air Museum at Iron Bridge. The station crane was removed there in 1973.

At Gnosall the embankments can be determined each side of the A518 on entering the village. The Shropshire Union Canal passes through Gnosall, linking Market Drayton and beyond to the north and Wolverhampton to the south. Gnosall's railway bridge across the A518 has gone but when in existence it carried the initials SUR (Shropshire Union Railways). The station too has gone, but happily components from the station's down booking office have been saved, to be found today at the

The ticket rack and booking office desk seen here at today's Blythe Bridge station on the preserved Foxfield Steam Railway came from Gnosall station on the Wellington to Stafford branch, which closed to passenger traffic in September 1964. (Photo Ian Rutherford)

121

Foxfield Railway at Caverswall Road station at Blythe Bridge in North Staffordshire. The ticket rack, booking office desk and window are all in use in the booking office.

The last station before Stafford was Haughton. Although the area has considerably increased in population over the last few decades, it still retains much of its rural character. The manor house with its close-timbered black and white building dates back to the 16th century, and the barn, now a cottage, boasts timbers reclaimed from sailing ships.

The Wellington to Stafford branch, like so many, fell victim to road competition and closed to passengers on 7th September 1964. Freight lingered awhile but was eventually discontinued between Newport and Stafford on 1st August 1966.

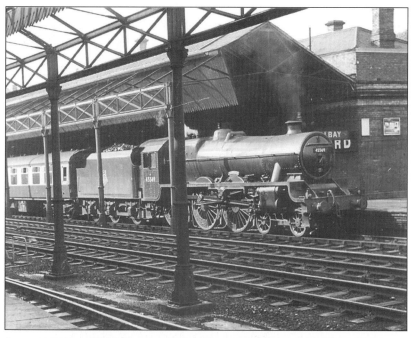

Locomotive no. 45569 Tasmania *hauls a passenger set at Stafford station, Whit-Monday 1953. The picture was taken before the rebuilding of the station building. (Russell Mulford)*

Wellington/Oakengates/Coalport (East)

The main aim of the LNWR branch from Wellington to Coalport was to break the GWR dominance of traffic in the industrial area to the south. The GWR had access to the ironworks and pits, whereas the LNWR had to make do with the Shropshire Canal, an independent branch of the Shropshire Union Canal, which ran from Trench to Coalport. The canal, however, was suffering badly from a shortage of water and subsidence and it was estimated that some £30,000 was needed for repairs. Rather than face this, the LNWR agreed in 1856 to build a single track branch from Wellington (Hadley junction) to Coalport.

The LNWR obtained powers to buy and convert part of the canal by an Act agreed on 27th July 1857. The line was built along the canal to a point east of Dawley and then winding southwards to Brookside and Tweedale and on to Coalport, adjacent to the River Severn. On the opposite bank of the river

A steam passenger train awaits departure at Coalport (East) station. Traffic was never heavy on the branch from Wellington and trains acquired the nickname 'The Coalport Dodgers'. (Lens of Sutton)

123

Ex-LMS 2-6-2T class 3P no. 40058 in steam at Coalport in the early BR days. The station name changed to Coalport (East) to avoid confusion with the GWR Coalport station across the river Severn. (Lens of Sutton)

Coalport (East) (ex-LMS) closed to passenger traffic in June 1952 but survived for freight until 1960. A BR (Swindon built) DMU passenger set visits the station with enthusiasts. (Lens of Sutton)

Wellington's Downside station building c.1950 when trains could be caught directly to Craven Arms, Stafford and beyond Market Drayton to Stoke. (Lens of Sutton)

some eight months later was to come the GWR Coalport station. This surely caused confusion for passengers, although it was clarified in later days when the LNWR station was renamed Coalport East. There were frequent plans to build a bridge across the river at Coalport but they never came to friution.

The single-track branch opened on 17th June 1861, although passenger traffic was never heavy. Trains took over half an hour to reach Coalport from Wellington, and the original third class fare was 8d for the whole journey. The trains gained the nick-name of the 'Coalport Dodgers'. The line's existence was mostly justified by its freight traffic. The branch became an early victim of road competition, with passenger traffic ending on 2nd June 1952. Goods traffic kept the branch alive for a further 12 years, a time when 'Cauliflower' 0-6-0s and Webb coal tanks were much in evidence.

Four miles of the former trackbed are today part of the 14-mile

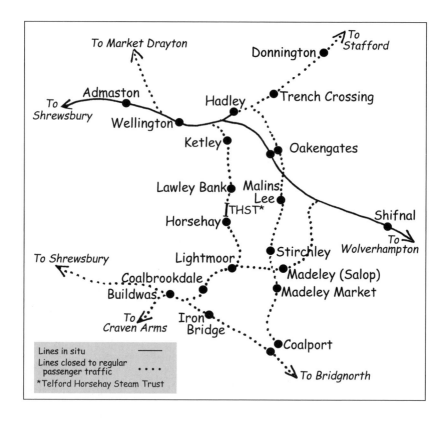

long Silkin Way, a walkway named in honour of Lord Silkin who pioneered Telford New Town. To the south, the Silkin Way leads to the Blists Hill Museum, which is part of the Ironbridge Gorge Museum. Here it is possible to see restored plateway trucks, the majority of which came from the Horsehay Ironworks.

11

GWR Lines at Much Wenlock and a Branch to Shifnal

Wellington/Lightmoor/Buildwas/
Much Wenlock/Craven Arms
Lightmoor/Madeley/Shifnal
Telford Horsehay Steam Trust

The line between Craven Arms and Much Wenlock closed to passengers in 1951 but the section northwards to Wellington lasted a further eleven years. Much Wenlock station building exists today as private properties (Lens of Sutton)

As early as the 16th century coal was exported from mines at Madeley and Broseley via the river Severn, and two centuries later traffic had reached 100,000 tons per year. In 1709 there came successful experiments when Abraham Darby (1677–1717) began to use coke made from local coal and not charcoal as a fuel to smelt iron. Cast-iron plate rails were constructed in 1767, representing a transitional stage between the thin wrought-iron plates previously in use and the edge rail that superseded them. The ironworks and collieries in the district continued to flourish through the 19th century, and, to improve transportation, the Shrewsbury & Birmingham Railway (S&BR) planned to bring a branch line into the area.

On 1st June 1854 a 4 mile freight line from west of Shifnal opened via Madeley and Lightmoor Platform to Coalbrookdale. Earlier, on 28th August 1853, the Wellington & Severn Junction Railway (W&SJR) had been authorised to build a line from Wellington to Lightmoor which would eventually link with the S&BR's branch from Shifnal.

The 'turning of the first sod' in August 1855 proved quite an event. A newspaper reported 'a series of festivities of the most joyous nature'. At an early hour on the great day, the people of Wellington woke to the firing of a cannon from the Shropshire Works. Later, folk were able to tour the vast works that constructed all the articles connected with the railway from 'the simple wood blocks to hold rails on the sleeper to the carriages which roll over them'.

At one o'clock there was a grand procession which included twelve navvies in white smocks carrying picks and shovels, a banner stating 'All Friends around the Wrekin' and another reading 'Success to the Wellington & Severn Junction Railway'. The ceremony was carried out in a field adjoining the S&BR, where Mr Williams, representing the contractor, dug up several sods, put them in a wheelbarrow, wheeled them along a plank and tipped them out at the end. There was much cheering, the National Anthem was played, and champagne corks popped.

The W&SJR opened to freight between Wellington and Horsehay Ironworks on 15th May 1857. By 1st August 1861 passenger services were available from Wellington to Coalbrookdale. Horsehay (known as Horsehay & Dawley) was the largest intermediate station. It had a busy yard with ten sidings, including two which served the Horsehay Ironworks. At Lightmoor passenger trains could reverse back on to the main S&BR line, using the existing

Horsehay & Dawley station c1910 on the branch from Wellington to Buildwas which closed to passengers in 1962. This picture was issued as a Christmas card – interesting but hardly seasonal! (Lens of Sutton)

freight line, opened in 1854, which provided a service via Madeley Court to Shifnal. The Lightmoor to Shifnal section survived for passengers only until 21st September 1925.

On 1st February 1862 the Severn Valley Railway opened providing four trains daily in each direction from Shrewsbury to join the main Birmingham to Worcester line at Hartlebury. On the same day, the Much Wenlock & Severn Junction Railway connected with services between Much Wenlock and Buildwas. All that remained to allow through services from Much Wenlock to Wellington was a rail connection across the river Severn between Buildwas and Coalbrookdale and this followed on 1st November 1864. The bridge across the river Severn, known as the Albert Edward Bridge, was constructed by the Coalbrookdale Company.

The final stretch of 14 miles to complete a through line from Wellington to Craven Arms was completed by the Wenlock railway (or to give it its full title – The Much Wenlock, Craven Arms and Coalbrookdale Company). From Much Wenlock the

Buildwas Junction where tracks to Craven Arms cross the line between Shrewsbury and Bridgnorth. It is here that passengers could change to catch trains on the Severn Valley Railway. (Lens of Sutton)

single track line met the Shrewsbury & Hereford Railway (S&HR) at Marsh Farm junction, north of Craven Arms. The line had been agreed by an Act of 1861 but it took over six years to complete, mainly because of local opposition from landowners at Presthope. This caused the railway to move from its originally planned course south of Wenlock Edge to tunnel through west of Presthope at considerable extra cost.

The line opened on 5th December 1864 as far as Presthope, where a temporary terminus was built. The remainder to Marsh Farm junction was completed on 16th December 1867, when trains could reach Craven Arms. Considerable improvements were made at Much Wenlock station, with the original station building becoming a goods shed. The sidings were numerous, and the small signal box had a potential of as many as 31 levers.

The entire branch was regarded as one of the most scenic in the British Isles, the journey giving fine views along the steeply graded sections. After leaving the main Wolverhampton line, trains climbed westward on a 1 in 50 gradient to reach Ketley, a

130

Much Wenlock station c1910. The town's first station was built in 1862 .as a terminus for trains arriving from Buildwas Junction. It was subsequently rebuilt to accommodate through traffic. (Lens of Sutton)

single platform with substantial buildings. Ketley Town Halt and New Dale Halt were followed by Lawley Bank, all opened in the 1930s to encourage local traffic. The gradient dropped sharply to 1 in 40 to reach Horsehay & Dawley, a rather gloomy station area improved only by the early summer show of rhododendrons along the opposite bank. Beyond Doseley Halt came Lightmoor junction, where the Madeley branch trailed in from the left. This was followed by Lightmoor Halt, which opened in 1907, then known as Lightmoor Platform, and of wooden and corrugated-iron construction.

Descending towards the river, trains passed Green Bank Halt and Coalbrookdale, where the famous iron works could be seen in the valley to the left. Coalbrookdale became a fully staffed station with a tiled platform and substantial brick buildings giving evidence of its importance. At Buildwas trains passed the (now demolished) Buildwas A Power Station. Beyond the river Severn the scenery became even more picturesque as trains made a steep and twisting ascent cutting through the limestone

131

in Farley Dingle to reach Wenlock Edge, a line of unbroken hills from Ironbridge to the Church Stretton Gap. Farley Halt opened in 1934, comprising a wooden shelter and platform, the area become busy during the Second World War when a siding led to a large underground petrol store.

Much Wenlock followed, a town of considerable historic importance with its attractive old houses and inns. As might be expected, the station building was constructed of imposing Gothic stone and there was a large and picturesque rockery on the opposite side of the single line. The station building remains very much in existence today, having been converted into private residences.

After climbing to Corve Dale, trains reached Westwood Halt (opened 1935) to then descend to the foot of Wenlock Edge at Presthope, the temporary terminus from 1864 to 1867. The line then passed through a tunnel (207 yds) to reappear at Easthope Halt (opened 1936). Longville and Rushbury both had sturdy

Although Longville closed to passengers in 1951, it remained open 'unofficially' for a further two years! Enthusiasts travelling on a 3-car DMU enjoy a break. (Lens of Sutton)

When visited by the author in 1992, Longville station was somewhat derelict.
Today it has been splendidly restored as a private residence. (Author)

red-brick buildings and the latter had a fine garden with ornamental fir trees. Longville station survives today, restored to
become a private residence. The station building at Rushbury also
lives on as a private residence. Rushbury nestles under Wenlock
Edge, in the valley of Apedale, sometimes referred to as 'The
Valley of the Bees'. This is because of the bee-keeping done in the
area by the monks of Wenlock Abbey during the 13th century. The
last station on the branch was Harton Road, after which the single
track joined the Shrewsbury to Hereford main line.

Around the turn of the century Wolverhampton-built 0-6-0
saddle tanks provided the motive power but from May 1906
steam railmotor units were used. These ran into difficulties on the
various gradients and were replaced a year later by 2-4-0 tanks,
although in later years class 44XX 2-6-2 tanks dominated the line.
In 1937 diesel railcars were tried but these also were defeated by
the gradients. As road competition increased, so passenger
receipts dropped, particularly on the Much Wenlock to Craven

133

Arms section. Often the pick-up freight between Longville and Craven Arms consisted of one solitary engine and brake van.

Sections of the Much Wenlock line were closed to passengers over a number of years from 31st December 1951. The first to go was the Much Wenlock to Craven Arms stretch, with the line between Longville and Marsh Farm junction closing to freight as well. A strange situation then arose, for, although services from Much Wenlock to Longville closed officially, passengers could continue to travel on to Longville for some two years afterwards. This came about because a parcel service remained in existence by extending the working of a passenger train from Wellington, and, guard willing, it was possible to travel on to Longville. Stranger still, perhaps, British Rail even marked the Much Wenlock–Longville section as open to passengers on some of its system maps!

Locomotive no. 1722 0-4-0ST (built by Peckett in 1926) leaves Spring Hill station for Horsehay and Dawley at the Telford Horsehay Steam Trust. Photograph taken Easter Sunday 20th April 2003. (Picture courtesy Alan Binns)

It is sad to reflect that when the Wellington–Buildwas–Much Wenlock section closed on 23rd July 1962, Much Wenlock station saw its busiest day. Over 200 people thronged the platform when the last passenger train left for Wellington at 7.05 pm. It was packed to capacity and was hauled by 2-6-2 tank locomotive no. 4178, which carried a board reading 'The Beeching Special'.

Telford Horsehay Steam Trust

The spirit of the earlier days of railways lives on today at the site of the former Horsehay & Dawley station where the Telford Steam Railway has its headquarters. The railway operates regular passenger trains, using many interesting and unique items of rolling stock. One fascinating display is an unusual, 2 ft-gauge steam tram, first sited at Telford Town Park and moved to its present location in 1988. This operates with a four-wheeled 12-seater vehicle with open third class accommodation. The site also has a miniature railway and an extensive model railway as well as other interesting railway memorabilia.

Telford Steam Railway has made great progress since it was established in 1976 with the assistance of the Telford Development Corporation. In May 1984 track was reopened between Horsehay Yard and Heath Hill Summit, and in December 1985 the line to Horsehay & Dawley station was reopened. In 2002 the line was extended to Heath Hill Tunnel. Currently the line is being extended northwards to a new terminus on Lawley Common, and track has been relaid to Doseley Halt.

The eventual aim of the railway and its owning company, Telford Horsehay Steam Trust, is to operate trains into the Ironbridge Gorge. This requires relaying the former GWR section between Doseley and Lightmoor junction and a bridge across the Ironbridge bypass and then joining the national rail network at the site of the former Lightmoor Halt, which closed in July 1962. Telford Steam Railway is operated entirely by volunteers and any offers of support by becoming a member of the Steam Trust will always be welcomed.

12

Lines Crossing County Borders

Wellington/Market Drayton/Nantwich
Market Drayton/Madeley Road/Stoke

Crudgington on the Wellington to Market Drayton branch. In this picture c.1910 station staff seem to outnumber passengers, although freight from a local creamery later proved profitable. (Lens of Sutton)

Wellington/Market Drayton/Nantwich

Wellington was once a town which boasted an important railway junction where many lines met. Apart from being on the main Shrewsbury to Birmingham route, branches carried trains on LNWR (later LMS) lines to Coalport and to Stafford, while

GWR branches led southwards to Much Wenlock and northwards to Market Drayton and on to Nantwich in Cheshire. This last route, now closed, wound its way across county borders and has been called a forgotten line, for today very little remains and nowhere along its route has any attempt been made to preserve any section.

Wellington (Salop) station, as it was known earlier, dates back to a time in 1849 when the Shrewsbury & Birmingham Railway was pressing eastwards to Birmingham. Originally, Wellington possessed a single platform, since which time an island platform was built on the up side and bays were added to accommodate Coalport and Much Wenlock trains. In the early 1900s Wellington station was a very different place from the present (renamed) Wellington Telford West station. There was much activity with upwards of 180 arrivals or departures of passing trains each weekday. The first train of the day was the 1.30 am Isle of Man boat express from Paddington, which called at Wellington at 5.07 am. Other important trains included the Cambrian express and daily south coast trains. One came from Birkenhead, travelling to Ramsgate, Dover and Deal, and another from Manchester via Crewe to reach Portsmouth. Expresses between Paddington and Birkenhead were frequent callers, often hauled by King or Castle locomotives and covering the journey between Wellington and Paddington in about three hours.

Subsequently, Wellington has seen many changes. Its engine shed, which housed mainly large Prairie tanks and panniers, closed in 1964, and, with the closure of the Coalport and Much Wenlock branches, numerous signal boxes were demolished. Its parcels office, once regularly crammed with bicycles, prams and the like, has gone, and the busy W.H. Smith bookstall is a thing of the past. The through daily south coast expresses, often with Southern Railway green coaches, have long been forgotten.

On 7th June 1861 Parliament approved the Nantwich & Market Drayton Railway. A year later, on 7th August 1862, the Wellington & Drayton Railway was incorporated. Both companies were GWR supported, as it considered the connections to be important, giving it access to both Crewe and Stoke-on-Trent.

There had previously been a number of unsuccessful schemes in the area, including the Sheffield, Shrewsbury & South Wales Direct Railway, which planned a route via Leek, Whitmore (crossing the main Crewe to Stafford line), Market Drayton and Hodnet. The GWR was anxious to thwart plans submitted. In addition the GWR opposed a proposal submitted by the Wellington & Cheshire Junction Railway for a line from Wellington to Market Drayton, Nantwich and Northwich.

Locomotive 45638 Zanzibar *hauls an express at Stoke, photographed on 17th September 1958. (D.K. Jones Collection)*

The 11 mile long branch from Nantwich to Market Drayton came first, opening on 20th October 1863 and four years later, on 16th October 1867, the Market Drayton to Wellington section of just over 16 miles was completed. The through route was classed as a secondary main line: stations were far apart and passengers were few. Three years later the North Staffordshire Railway (NSR) reached Market Drayton from Stoke, a line which served the industrial areas west of Stoke-on-Trent.

Travelling northwards from Wellington, trains branched away from the main Shrewsbury line, past Admaston to Bratton. The latter is the most northerly point of the 14 mile long Silkin Way walkway which crossed Telford New Town from the river Severn. The first intermediate station was Crudgington, close to where the rivers Strine and Tern meet. In the early 1920s a farmers' co-operative was set up at Crudgington, sending milk to London in the winter and making cheese in the summer. It became a true creamery, collecting only cream for butter making, and was taken over by the Milk Marketing Board in 1935. Today

Peplow station not long before closure. Like many along the branch, it was sited in a very rural area and saw few passengers. (Lens of Sutton)

139

the complex of buildings houses a Research and Development establishment as well as being a depot with packaging units trading under the well known brand name Dairy Crest. Beyond Crudgington came Peplow station, serving a truly rural area of scattered farms which could hardly have attracted many passengers.

The next station, Hodnet, had its busiest days on Tuesdays when both GWR and NSR trains arrived with passengers coming to the market. The NSR trains came from Stoke via Market Drayton, having been extended over GWR tracks to avoid a two hour wait at Market Drayton for a connection. At Tern Hill trains crossed the river Tern by a low three-arched bridge. The station was sited where the A53 crosses the A41, an overbridge on the latter having been demolished since closure to allow a road improvement. Passengers were few, although there was additional traffic in the early 1920s when a large aerodrome was established nearby.

Looking northwards towards Market Drayton at Peplow station. Although the station closed in September 1963 to passengers, it remained open a further two years for freight traffic. (Lens of Sutton)

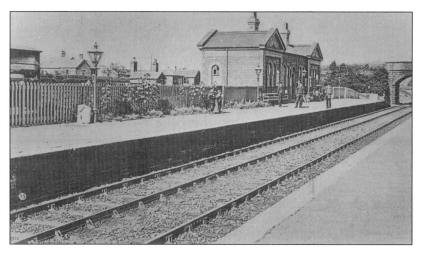

Hodnet station, which was served by GWR trains and also by North Staffordshire Railway (NSR) trains from Stoke. Many passengers came to Hodnet to visit Hodnet Hall, well-known for its lakeside gardens. (Lens of Sutton)

Market Drayton derived the first part of its name from the markets that have been held there for over 750 years. Each Wednesday visitors can join in a bustling, bargain-hunting tradition in traffic-free streets and under the old buttercross. One of the town's celebrated products is gingerbread, faithful to recipes up to 200 years old and made by the local bakers' shops.

There were only two intermediate stations between Market Drayton and Nantwich, these being Adderley and Audlem. Adderley station served nearby Adderley Hall, and it was near Audlem that the railway criss-crossed the Shropshire-Cheshire border. Audlem is perhaps better known today for its canal and series of locks. It is recorded that Moss Hall (near Audlem station) had three subterranean passages entered through secret doors. These were reputed to be places used by the family living at the Hall to hide from Cromwell's army.

In the early 1920s there were six stopping trains each way on weekdays between Wellington and Nantwich, and only one on Sunday. In an effort to increase passenger traffic in the early

141

*Audlem station on the Market Drayton to Nantwich branch, an area better
known today for its canal and locks. When traffic dwindled on the branch
in the early 1930s, the GWR opened halts but it made little difference.
(Late Tony Birch, Birch-Holland Collection, courtesy Mark Smith)*

1930s, the GWR opened seven halts but it did little to help. The
line became considerably busier during electrification of the
main line from London through Crewe and for a time its
prospects looked good. But this did not last, and the familiar
downward trend followed. Passenger services survived until 9th
September 1963. Freight services lasted only another four years.

A final indignity came to the branch when it was suggested
that the Market Drayton to Nantwich stretch might become a
walkway. Whereas the short section from Wellington to Bratton
became part of the Silkin Way, local authorities in Cheshire were
less co-operative, considering the trackbed to be unsuitable.

Market Drayton/Madeley Road/Stoke

There was a time when the village of Norton-in-Hales, close to the Shropshire and Staffordshire borders, boasted three public houses and shops which included a butcher's, a general stores and a laundry. Not far away, where the lane climbed over the single-track railway line, could be found Norton-in-Hales station. The station building is still there, plus part of the original awning, which had been restored from derelict. Special trains used to run from Stoke, bringing large crowds to the village for the annual harvest festivals, and afterwards the Market Drayton Town Band played whilst a meal was provided under canvas in the rectory grounds.

Norton-in-Hales was one of the intermediary stations on a line opened on 1st February 1870 by the North Staffordshire Railway

Norton-in-Hales station on the North Staffordshire Railway line between Market Drayton and Stoke. The line closed to passengers in May 1956 and the station building is now a private residence. (Late Tony Birch, Birch-Holland Collection, courtesy Mark Smith)

from Stoke to Market Drayton. As this was not the first railway to reach Market Drayton, celebrations were somewhat muted. In the book *The Stoke to Market Drayton Line*, C. R. Lester wrote of the various festivities that did take place. A commemorative public ball was held at the Corbet Arms assembly rooms in Market Drayton, and at Pipe Gate visitors from Silverdale were among the 30 guests who celebrated the occasion with a dinner at the Chetwode Arms Inn. The toast was 'Success to the North Staffordshire Railway', and when the last train left Pipe Gate for Stoke at 8.35 pm few were on it. One may assume celebrations lasted well into the night, with a number of bleary-eyed passengers on the 10.45 am the next morning.

Four trains ran each way on weekdays and two on Sunday, with intermediate stations initially between Market Drayton and Stoke at Norton-in-Hales, Pipe Gate (for Pipe Gate and Woore) and Keele (for Keele and Madeley). As well as providing a useful passenger service and agricultural links, it was expected the line

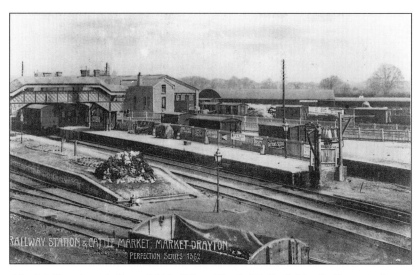

Market Drayton station c.1910. When North Staffordshire Railway trains reached the town in 1870, it was initially more an intention to keep GWR trains out of their area rather than provide a service. (Lens of Sutton)

144

would further develop collieries and bring North Staffordshire into direct communication with GWR lines. Also the need for half-day excursions out of Stoke turned Norton-in-Hales into a health resort and it soon became popular with tourists looking for a country outing or as a place for Sunday School treats.

With the arrival of NSR trains, the original passenger station at Market Drayton was enlarged. It was rebuilt in a French Renaissance style with ornamental ironwork and square-topped pavilions at each end. In later years NSR trains were operated via Market Drayton on GWR tracks to Hodnet on market days and often further south to places beyond Wellington. Madeley station, described as a 'small wayside station', opened later between Keele and Pipe Gate. For a short time during 1871 Madeley station was known as Madeley Manor, later to become Madeley Road for the rest of its life.

Pipe Gate became busy with trade in timber and cattle, and in the 1880s a creamery and milk condensing plant was

Market Drayton station not long before closure. NSR passenger services from Stoke came to an end in 1956 but GWR trains between Wellington and Nantwich lasted until 1963. (Lens of Sutton)

145

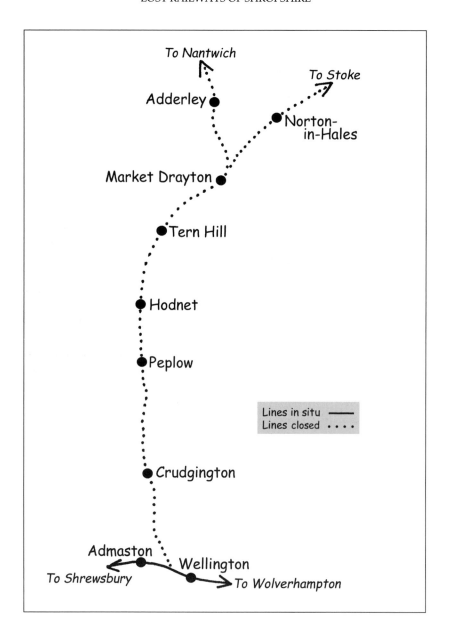

established. Services to Pipe Gate increased considerably when, in 1885, a racecourse was laid out on farmland about half a mile to the north of the station. Race trains came from many Midlands towns and extra staff were drafted in to cope with the crowds. Towards Stoke a small station called Keele Park was opened when a steeplechase course was constructed. Training and breeding stables were set up nearby and a horse loading dock was built at Keele station. The racecourse lasted until 1901, when finances deteriorated.

In 1905 a Beyer Peacock railcar was introduced to the Market Drayton branch as an economy measure. Further halts were opened in an effort to attract passengers, but, as the 1920s progressed, competition from road transport took its toll. To compete, the NSR (now LMS) provided additional trains but it was in vain. Early in 1956 British Rail announced closure of the line from Market Drayton to Silverdale, and, despite efforts by a local transport users' consultative committee, the end for passenger traffic came on Saturday, 5th May.

As usual for a final day, the train carried its heaviest load for many years. As 2-6-4T locomotive no. 42671 hauled four coaches from Market Drayton at 7 pm, the occasion was marked by exploding detonators. Along the line, small groups of mourners watched the passing. Eighty-six years of service had come to an end, although passenger services between the Silverdale and Stoke section lasted a further eight years until closure on 2nd March 1964.

Conclusion

The decline of many branches began in Britain in the 1920s. Buses were able to offer a more flexible service than trains, and road haulage was on the increase. In addition, the private motor car was beginning to make its presence felt. After nationalisation in 1948, the railways, still recovering from the demands of war service, were slow to meet any competition and were losing ground. Reduced revenue was leading to increased economies and then closures, with the entire pattern of inland transport gradually changing.

An early closure in Shropshire was the short branch from Lightmoor to Shifnal on the main Shrewsbury to Wolverhampton line, which ceased passenger traffic in September 1925. Later, in November 1933, the 'Potts line', as it was known, closed to regular passenger services. After the Second World War, many more lines came to grief.

In March 1963 proposals were made in a report which became popularly known as the 'Beeching Plan'. Basically the idea was to keep lines considered suitable to rail traffic and give up the remainder. It was claimed that one third of the rail system in Britain carried only 1% of the total traffic! Further drastic cuts inevitably followed and many more lines disappeared. Closures – at first a trickle – became a torrent. Where branches once existed, some linking major routes across the region, soon only the original trunk routes remained. A few branch lines have survived but their future must surely be considered as uncertain.

What does the future hold for Shropshire? There has been talk of reopening sections of the former Cambrian/GWR line between Oswestry and Blodwell Junction and then on to Nantmawr. Much of the track still exists and, although mothballed, it is very overgrown. This would have to be brought up to standard to meet safety levels. Similarly, plans have been considered to reach Llanymynech from Oswestry. A section of track south of Llynclys has already been relaid and rolling stock added. But much more needs to be done. Track still survives, too, between Oswestry and Gobowen, and there has also been talk of reopening this link, connecting Oswestry to the main Shrewsbury to Chester line and beyond. Another plan exists to reopen a line from Wellington to Donnington, where a railfreight terminus could be created near the Donnington MOD base. The track was removed only a year or so ago. Furthermore, attempts are being considered to reopen closed stations. An example is Baschurch on the busy Shrewsbury to Chester line, which closed to passengers in 1960. Why a station in such a populated area ever closed is hard to understand.

From the days of Shropshire's early turnpikes and tollgates, time has taken us through the canal age to the railway age. 'Railway mania' is now well behind us and we are back to the roads once again, with cars and motorways a part of present day life. Yet many roads and motorways are already quite inadequate for the task intended, with lorries continually increasing in weight and the volume of traffic reaching ever higher proportions. Surely those who closed down so many of our branch lines have much to answer for.

At the present time continuing financial losses on the railways appear inevitable. Perhaps there is comfort in the fact that further widespread closures on the scale previously suffered would be politically unacceptable today. Presumably government subsidies will continue and will, no doubt, increase in the years to come. It is difficult to foresee the railway's future. One of the main disadvantages is that this is in the hands of politicians. Sadly the days have gone when the railways provided an efficient service throughout and when railway employees could take a real pride in the job.

Opening and Final Closure Dates of Lines to Regular Passenger Traffic

Line	Opened	Final Closure
Oswestry/Gobowen	12 Oct 1848	7 Nov 1966
Wellington/Newport/Stafford	1 June 1849	7 Sep 1964
Oswestry/Welshpool	14 Aug 1860	18 Jan 1965
Shrewsbury/Pontesbury/ Minsterley	14 Feb 1861	5 Feb 1951
Wellington/Oakengates/ Coalport (East)	17 Jun 1861	2 Jun 1952
Wellington/Coalbrookdale	1 Aug 1861	23 Jul 1962
Lightmoor/Shifnal	1 Aug 1861	21 Sep 1925 *1
Woofferton/Tenbury Wells	1 Aug 1861	31 Jul 1961
Shrewsbury/Coalport/ Bridgnorth/Bewdley	1 Feb 1862	9 Sep 1963 *2
Bewdley/Hartlebury	1 Feb 1862	5 Jan 1970
Buildwas/Much Wenlock	1 Feb 1862	23 Jul 1962
Llanymynech/Llanfyllin	17 Jul 1863	18 Jan 1965
Market Drayton/Nantwich	20 Oct 1863	9 Sep 1963
Oswestry/Whitchurch	27 Jul 1864	18 Jan 1965
Tenbury Wells/Bewdley	13 Aug 1864	1 Aug 1962
Ludlow/Bitterley	24 Aug 1864	31 Dec 1962
Coalbrookdale/Buildwas	1 Nov 1864	23 Jul 1962
Much Wenlock/Presthope	5 Dec 1864	31 Dec 1951
Craven Arms/Stretford Bridge/ Lydham Heath/Bishop's Castle	1 Feb 1866	20 Apr 1935
Shrewsbury/Kinnerley/ Llanymynech	13 Aug 1866	6 Nov 1933 *3
Wellington/Market Drayton	16 Oct 1867	9 Sep 1963

Presthope/Craven Arms	16 Dec 1867	31 Dec 1951
Market Drayton/Stoke	1 Feb 1870	5 May 1956[*4]
Kinnerley/Criggion	2 Jun 1871	6 Nov 1933
Bewdley/Kidderminster	1 Jun 1878	3 Jan 1970
Ellesmere/Wrexham	2 Nov 1895	10 Sep 1962
Welshpool/Llanfair Caereinion	4 Apr 1903	7 Feb 1931[*5]
Porth-y-waen/Llangynog (Tanat Valley)	5 Jan 1904	5 Feb 1951
Cleobury Mortimer/Ditton Priors	21 Nov 1908	26 Sep 1938

[*1] The Shifnal to Lightmoor branch closed to passengers from March 1915 to July 1925. The line finally closed to passengers 21st September 1925.

[*2] Steam trains recommenced at Bridgnorth on 23rd May 1970 when the Severn Valley Railway Society started limited services. Services from Bridgnorth to Kidderminster started on 30th July 1984.

[*3] Shrewsbury to Llanymynech was reopened by the War Department during World War II. Final closure on 29th Feb 1960.

[*4] A section of the Market Drayton to Stoke line between Silverdale and Stoke survived until 2nd March 1964.

[*5] Steam trains recommenced when the Welshpool & Llanfair Light Railway Preservation Society reopened a section opened between Llanfair Caereinion and Castle Caereinion on 6th April 1963. Trains were restored along the entire route between Llanfair Caereinion and Welshpool Raven Square on 18th July 1981.

Bibliography

In compiling **Lost Railways of Shropshire**, I have referred to numerous sources, many now out of print, which include the following that can be recommended for further reading:

Author	Title	Publisher
Rex Christiansen	*Forgotten Railways: Severn Valley and Welsh Border*	David & Charles
Rex Christiansen	*The West Midlands North and Mid Wales*	David & Charles
Rex Christiansen	*A Regional History of the Railways of Great Britain Vol 7 The West Midlands*	David & Charles
Peter E. Baughan	*A Regional History of the Railways of Great Britain Vol 11 North and Mid Wales*	David & Charles
R W Kidner	*The Cambrian Railways*	The Oakwood Press
Mike Lloyd	*The Tanat Valley Light Railway*	Wild Swan Publications Ltd
Eric S. Tonks	*The Shropshire & Montgomeryshire Railway*	The Industrial Railway Society
Keith & Susan Turner	*The Shropshire & Montgomeryshire Light Railway*	David & Charles

Eric S. Tonks	*The Snailbeach District Railways*	The Industrial Railway Society
Edward Griffith	*The Bishop's Castle Railway 1865–1935*	Edward Griffith
W. Smith and K. Beddoes	*The Cleobury Mortimer and Ditton Priors Light Railway*	Oxford Publishing Co
C. R. Lester	*The Stoke to Market Drayton Line*	The Oakwood Press

Index